KEEPING YOUR NERVE!

REFERENCE ONLY

Kate Jones

FABER **ff** MUSIC

© 2000 by Kate Jones
First published in 2000 by Faber Music Ltd
Bloomsbury House
74–77 Great Russell Street
London WC1B 3DA
Illustrations by Harry Venning
Design by Nick Flower
Printed in England by Caligraving Ltd

ISBN10: 0-571-51922-9
EAN13: 978-0-571-51922-4

To buy Faber Music publications or to find out about
the full range of titles available please contact your
local music retailer or Faber Music sales enquiries:

Sales Department, Faber Music Ltd,
Burnt Mill, Elizabeth Way, Harlow. CM20 2HX
Tel: +44 (0)1279 82 89 82
Fax: +44 (0)1279 82 89 83
sales@fabermusic.com
fabermusic.com

Contents

Kate Jones works as a counsellor for musicians. She studied music at Goldsmith's College, University of London (first study flute), and has as an MA in African music, art and religions from the School of Oriental and African Studies, University of London.

For the last ten years she has worked as an arts press and marketing consultant, running her own company, Classical Communications, and working as a Press Officer for Philips Classics, Collins Classics and BBC Radio 3. She has also worked in radio, edited a magazine, sung in the London Symphony Chorus, and practised as a reflexologist. She lives in Herefordshire with her husband and a growing number of animals!

Acknowledgements

I would like to thank the following for their help in my research for this book: Christine Brown, Elvis Costello, Richard Crozier, Steven Isserlis, Stephen Kovacevich, Christian Lindberg, Joanna MacGregor, Lin Marsh, Suzannah Power and Gillian Weir. I would also like to thank my editor, Ben Warren, and my husband, Stephen Johnson, for their generous support and encouragement.

Introduction

The lights dim and silence falls. You walk out on to the stage, head up, confident. You bow to the audience and start to play. Everything seems to be going according to plan. Then suddenly your body is wildly out of control. Your hands are cold and wet, your knees are shaking. The pounding in your chest drowns out all other sounds and the world around you begins to swim out of focus. All the nerves you have felt over the last week condense into one feeling—panic.

A familiar story? Well, you are not alone. These are the classic signs of performance nerves. There is, however, something you can do about it. It is possible to use those same nerves to your advantage. Interested? Then read on.

When I started to write this book, I had a horrible recollection of being fourteen again. I can remember so vividly all those dreadful feelings before a concert or an exam. In my case, my performance nerves were so bad that I gave up on my dream of being a professional flautist half-way through university. I am now an active amateur musician and, although I still get nervous, I know better how to work with my nerves and, more importantly, how to enjoy myself when playing or singing. This book, therefore, is for all amateur musicians. It is also for teachers and parents in their role as a support to those performing.

One of the most important things I have learned over the years is that I am not alone. When I was in my teens there was so much pressure to succeed that I never told anyone how I was feeling. If only I had been able to talk to someone, I could have understood why I was getting so nervous. And if we understand why something happens, it usually becomes less frightening.

Chapter 2 looks briefly at some of the causes of performance nerves. Because nerves are an intrinsic part of human nature, a lot of research has been done over the years into harnessing stress and turning it into a positive force. You can reap the benefits of this research in Chapter 3, which gives some practical ideas for coping with the build-up to the 'big day'.

I now know that even the most famous musicians suffer or have suffered from performance nerves at some stage in their career. In Chapter 4 you will find out how the professionals cope with the difficulties posed by their own instrument, be it piano, saxophone, cello, trombone or voice.

Chapter 5 is designed mainly for parents and teachers. It is full of practical advice from experienced teachers about how best to help and support your child or pupil without exerting too much pressure. The issue of 'passing' and 'failing' is complicated and it is vital to get it in perspective. In music-making there is no pass or fail, only performing as well as you can on the day.

Chapter 6 looks at how to learn from the experience of performance nerves and how to achieve a state of relaxed concentration in both exams and public performance. However, I don't want to lose sight of the fact that there are millions of people out there whose motivation for making music is enjoyment pure and simple. Chapter 7 examines why we perform and how best to enjoy the experience.

It may well be that not all the ideas in this book are relevant to you, because everyone is different, but you will find plenty of suggestions here to help you keep your nerve and enjoy what you do—which is to make music.

Nerves, stress, tension, anxiety—these words are in constant use nowadays; the damage that they can cause, both physically and mentally, is written about endlessly in magazines and newspapers, and discussed on radio and television. Yet somehow we performers often ignore all the advice that is being given. Because of the special nature of what we do, the tips about how to cope with stress can seem far removed from our situation. In fact, the physical and mental manifestations of nerves and anxiety are the same for everybody; the problem for performers is that they are counter-productive to the task at hand: performing in front of an audience.

This is when understanding what is going on can be helpful.

1. Our bodies are not really designed for concert performance. They are designed for survival: finding food and shelter, maintaining body warmth, and coping with life-threatening situations.

Our bodies are designed for survival …

2. This dealing with life-threatening situations is responsible for something we all learned about in biology at school (and then instantly forgot!), the 'fight or flight reaction'. In a stressful situation our bodies react in an instinctive and dramatic way.

3. Our mental alertness is increased, but it becomes channelled into avoiding or coping with danger. It does not help us to think clearly and profoundly about the music, it homes in on how to get us out of this stressful situation—fast! Hence the tendency to rush the performance in order to 'get it over with'.

4. Our tactile senses sharpen (enabling us to do things better and faster) and the palms of our hands and soles of our feet start to perspire. Fine if you're being chased by a lion in the jungle, not very helpful on the concert platform or in the exam room.

5. The body also reacts to protect itself from injury by restricting the amount of blood that goes to the surface of the body. This leaves more blood available for the major organs and the larger muscles ready for 'fight or flight'. The result is cold hands and restricted use of the smaller muscles of the body, such as those necessary for fine coordination of the hands, eyes and ears.

6. Finally all the muscles of the body tense up, ready for the final 'fight or flight'. Tense muscles create more strength and better protection from injury. In this state you could probably carry the piano out of the room all by yourself—but as for using those muscles to perform complex and intricate tasks, you might as well forget it.

7. There are also the mental and emotional responses to anxiety: the fear of failure, the constant comparisons with

your fellow musicians, the feeling of letting everyone down, and the often very real fear that everyone will know how nervous you are and that this somehow lessens you as a human being. These feelings will feed on the associated physical problems and the results can be even more devastating, particularly since they often kick in weeks before the performance.

8. The symptoms of nerves can be put into three categories: **physiological**—the physical symptoms such as rapid heartbeat, sweating, cold hands, shaking, etc.; **cognitive**—worrying about unpleasant things happening, coupled with an inability to think clearly; and **behavioural**—not being able to do things which normally come naturally (such as breathing or walking), and avoiding doing or thinking about things which may provoke anxiety (for example, refusing to think far enough ahead in order to give yourself enough practice time). Just knowing that the symptoms of nerves are normal can lessen anxiety.

9. It is also important to remember that nerves and tension can actually be useful, and that sometimes we are tense and nervous without even knowing it. Think of the tension in an audience waiting for a performance to begin. The feeling of excitement and anticipation is stimulating to you as the performer as well as to the audience, and it can add enormously to the musical experience all round.

10. If you can learn to accept and master this tension, you may then find a way of expressing it through the music to dramatic effect. But this tension must also be balanced by relaxation. In physics the word tension means 'stretching': a pulling of particles away from each other, balanced by

the forces of cohesion drawing them together. The all-important word here is balance. The tension created must be balanced by relaxation.

11. A lot can be learned from just listening to music: how the moments of dramatic tension are balanced by passages of relaxation; how the tension mounts towards a climax and is then released in its resolution. If this can be translated into your performance, then everyone will go home happy.

12. Your audience, whoever they are—friends, family, the examiner, the school governors or even a group of music critics—are human and they want to enjoy the experience too. If they sense that you are having a good time, that will encourage them to believe in what you are doing.

During the course of this book you will find lots of ideas to help you cope with performance nerves. Many of the tips and relaxation techniques suggested by the experts have been tried and tested by professional musicians. So now that we know what's going on when we get nervous, and we know that it can sometimes help to be nervous, let's look at some practical advice on how to harness those nerves to your advantage.

The day is looming. You are experiencing that uncomfortable feeling of time moving faster. The date on the calendar which had seemed a long way off is suddenly only weeks away. That familiar feeling of panic is beginning to kick in.

It's all very well knowing the theory of fear; the big question is how to combat it. So sit down, take a few deep breaths and have a look at the following advice.

General preparation

The most important aspect of your performance is that you can actually play—or, if you are a singer, sing—the music. It is vital that you have the technical ability to do so. If you can't play the music, the nervousness you are feeling will automatically increase, because you know that when you get to page 22, bar 17, or whichever passage it is, you can't do it. The process of technical preparation, therefore, is one of the key elements in eliminating nerves.

1. Prepare well in advance. It is vital to draw up a realistic practice schedule and stick to it. Practising in small chunks is far more effective than in one or two big sessions. But don't forget to reward yourself when you have achieved what you intended.

2. The timescale of your practice is important. You may need to practise something many times to get it right. But you also need to leave time to let what you have learned sink in. Leave time and space around the performance. Any 'practice' you try to cram in just before you go on stage will only be counter-productive.

3. If you are not a pianist, try and make sure you have as much practice with your accompanist as possible. It's important that you know the accompaniment as well. After all, it is part of the music! And don't be afraid of your accompanist. You are the soloist and they are there to make music with you. The same goes for ensemble playing. Getting to know your colleagues and how they may deal with nerves is as important as practising the notes.

Don't be afraid of your accompanist ...

4. If you are playing several pieces in your recital and you are able to devise the programme order, it is often helpful to start with a piece you know well or a piece that isn't too technically demanding. This way you allow yourself the best warming-up conditions and are more likely to control your nerves.

5. Make sure you like the music you are playing. Enjoying what you do is another key element to reducing any nerves you may feel. It's your performance and you need to be in control.

6. Get to know the venue. If you can, visit it well in advance. See if it's possible to try out the piano. Find out what music stands are used and how to adjust them. Try walking into the room or on to the stage so you know how that feels.

7. Decide if you need support on the performance or exam day. If you do need support, make sure it's the right person. There's nothing worse than someone who makes you feel more nervous.

8. Allow plenty of time to get to the venue, as you can never predict what might happen en route. Equally, have a contingency plan so that if you arrive early you are not just sitting around. See if there is a park or a café nearby where you could use any spare time you have doing something not connected with the impending performance. Above all, use the time to relax.

Allow plenty of time to get to the venue, as you can never predict what might happen en route …

9. When you finally get on stage, take your time to make sure everything is how you want it. If you are a pianist, check the height of the stool. If you are using a music stand, make sure it's in the right position for you. This kind of preparation will not only give you a moment's breathing space, but also convince your audience that you are in control.

Mind and body

All of the above advice is very practical. To do well on the day, you will also need to pay attention to two less tangible aspects: your mind and your body.

1. Remember that performance—whether it is taking an exam or appearing in front of an audience—is what making music is all about. In one sense it's not a 'big day' at all, it is simply part of your life. Take every opportunity to play in front of your friends, family or neighbours. If you make a mistake, keep going. Often they won't even notice!

2. Be aware of your body. Work out what and when it's best to eat. Beware of the effects of stimulants such as tea and coffee. Find out whether you like to be quiet when you are nervous or whether a bit of distraction helps.

3. Physical fitness and mental fitness go hand in hand. Physical exercise is vital for improving stamina as well as relaxing those tense limbs. And you will probably find that exercise helps to clear your mind and put things in perspective. Try to do some form of physical exercise every day, even if it's just a short walk.

4. Understanding that your mind and body are linked is crucial in helping to overcome performance nerves. Many professional musicians (as well as world-class athletes) use a variety of relaxation activities which work on the mind as well as the body. See what opportunities there are in your area for Alexander Technique, yoga, massage, reflexology, t'ai chi or aikido.

5. One of the most commonly used relaxation techniques doesn't involve going to a class at all. Simply lie on your back on the floor, making sure you are warm and comfortable. Allow your feet to flop out and your hands to fall loosely at your sides. Close your eyes and start to concentrate on your breathing. Try to breathe a little more deeply. Then start to think about the various parts of the body, starting with your toes. Are they relaxed? To find out, tense them and then relax them—you'll soon see the difference. Once you have relaxed all of your body, come back to your breathing and breathe slowly and deeply for five to ten minutes, concentrating on the gentle rhythm as you breathe in and then out. When you are ready to get up, gently wiggle your toes and fingers and bring your mind back to your body. Finally,

This relaxation technique only requires you to lie down ...

remember to treat yourself gently as you turn on to your side and get up.

6. By freeing the body through simple relaxation techniques, you can improve your mental abilities. If the body is relaxed, there will be less interference in the nerves going to the brain. This means that your mind will be capable of greater memory and concentration—vital in the stressful situation of performance.

7. Freedom of movement counteracts nervousness. Just think how people pace up and down when they're nervous and how being stuck in one place or position adds to tension. If you watch any folk or jazz musicians, there is far more movement in their playing. Try experimenting with this in your daily practice as well as in performance.

8. Some musicians prepare their bodies a few days in advance of a performance by simulating the difficulties of playing under stress, the idea being that they will then be better able to cope on the day. Try running up and down stairs and then attempt to play. This will reproduce the feeling of breathlessness that so often takes us by surprise. Another trick is to try playing in a really hot environment so that you get used to the problems caused by excessive perspiration; alternatively, try playing in a cold one—this should prepare you for any eventuality!

We've looked at ways of preparing for the performance and reducing pre-performance nerves. In the next chapter, let's see how the professionals do it, and how they cope with nerves once they're actually on stage.

In this chapter I have interviewed the following well-known musicians: pianists Joanna MacGregor and Stephen Kovacevich, cellist Steven Isserlis, singer Elvis Costello, trombonist Christian Lindberg, and organist Gillian Weir.

Most professional musicians I meet experience some form of performance nerves. Some were crippled by them and found ways of coping. Others still suffer and simply accept them as part of their lives. Most performers get nervous before a concert to a greater or lesser extent but have developed ways of dealing with it.

Handling performance nerves is as much about your attitude of mind as it is about practical solutions. I talked to a range of well-known musicians about how they learned not only to accept but also to value nerves as part of life as a musician. They talk about the different problems posed by their instrument and give some hints from their experience on how to cope with those anxious hours before a performance.

General preparation

Understanding that nerves are necessary is a vital step towards coping with them. The cellist Steven Isserlis believes that 'it's a bad sign if musicians aren't nervous at all, it can often give a blasé feel to the performance. I do recognize that nerves give my performance a certain extra adrenalin, even if they do make me suffer.' Trombonist Christian Lindberg agrees: 'I think you have to have a certain tension in yourself to make an interesting performance. Nerves create excitement in the hall.' Pianist Stephen Kovacevich agrees, but sees different kinds or levels of nervousness: 'Some nerves do make you hotter and you do play with a special fire. But if you are so nervous that your hands are frozen, you will only communicate fear.' Joanna MacGregor feels the same: 'Being alert, being alive to the situation—it's different from the kind of nerves which prevent you from functioning.'

Remember that the music is the most important thing. Steven Isserlis suffers from cold hands before a concert, but he tries to ignore them: 'Performing is not about having warm hands or hitting every note, it's about conveying the music. You can't hope for miracles, you can only do your best. Listen to the music and try to convey that.' Joanna MacGregor believes this was one of the keys to her becoming less nervous: 'The moment that I began to lose some of my nerves was when I started working with composers. Then it wasn't about comparing myself to other pianists, it was about communicating what the composers were writing. My playing became uniquely about communicating music and nothing else.'

Singer and song-writer Elvis Costello knows the importance of believing that the audience is on your side: 'The chances are that 90 per cent of the audience don't know how

Some people believe it's a bad sign if musicians aren't nervous at all …

to play the piece you're playing. I've never been to a concert where people are impatient with the performer. You have the benefit of their goodwill—unless you do something to cause this to evaporate, like becoming arrogant.' Organist Dame Gillian Weir agrees: 'Remember the audience are there because they want a pleasant evening with some marvellous music. You are their guide in this tour through the land of music. They are not there to find fault and criticize. If there *are* some critical people who, you imagine, want you to go wrong, then the odd wrong note here or there will make them happy, so you will have pleased somebody even then!'

Stephen Kovacevich, a pianist who suffered from nerves for a large part of his career, also believes that what attracts the audience is the element of danger. He likens concert performance to a high-wire circus act: 'Why are people thrilled by great virtuosity? Because inherent in it are great risks. And what's wonderful is to play without a net.' Joanna MacGregor takes a more pragmatic approach to the thrill of live performance: 'If you expect to feel normal then of course you'll be very alarmed. You are not going to feel normal because you are about to do something which isn't normal. I think that's the confusion for a lot of young people, because they feel jumpy and then they feel all sorts of twinges, and rather than thinking, "This is an absolute nightmare, what can I do to get rid of these feelings?" you need to start thinking, "This is OK, this is quite natural and normal. I'm feeling alert and ready to go."'

The creation of unrealistic expectations can be dangerous. Christian Lindberg firmly believes that the seriousness of the classical music business and the perfection required on CDs has a lot to answer for: 'The pressure for people to be correct in every single situation and not to make any mistakes when playing incredibly difficult works is impossible. In performance what you need to say to yourself if you make a split note is "It doesn't matter."' Joanna MacGregor agrees and believes that a lot of nerves are caused by the pressure of competition and judgement as we go through our training. She was helped enormously by something someone once said to her: '"When you perform, it's the most important thing in the world to you and at the same time it is not important at all. People are not going to die, the world isn't going to stop turning." If you can really grasp this, it gives you a sense of proportion. Performance is about communicating the music, it's not about proving how good you are or humiliating yourself. If you do muck things up, try to find a way of forgiving yourself. Try saying, "Okay, so this time I mucked that bar up, I hit a wrong note. Next time it won't happen." At the time it does matter,

Performance is like a high-wire circus act …

but you've got to try and be a bigger person than the one bar you are agonizing over.

For Stephen Kovacevich understanding himself better was a vital key: 'Two factors helped me get over my nerves. One was getting older and not caring so much—a degree of indifference is like gold, but of course you can't pretend to be indifferent. And the other thing that helped me was when I discovered that at some point in my youth I had not felt entitled to my own feelings. If I had felt accepted as a child for everything that I did and however well or badly I played, then I may not have developed such appalling nerves. If you can be reassured about yourself as a person, that's very important. People who are comfortable with themselves have more of a chance of surviving.'

Elvis Costello, however, feels that physical exercise and relaxation are very important: 'I do stretching exercises every morning, I go swimming and when I'm at home I try to play tennis as often as I can. Sometimes I think, "I should really be practising", but I get more out of the preparation time I do put aside because I did some other kind of activity and didn't become too obsessively focused on practising.'

Joanna MacGregor has some sound advice on one particular problem of being a pianist—that is, preparing to play on a different piano from your own: 'You have to expect it to be different. You have to say, "This is not going to be like the piano I normally play on. It may have some annoying bits to it, but it may also have some things which it does better than my own piano." Sometimes you get a piano which is a real dog and that's all there is to it. It's good if you can get into the habit of enjoying playing bad pianos. It's important not to panic from your first impressions of a new piano. Give the piano a chance—what may seem very odd for the first few minutes may feel OK after a while. The other thing is to try and project yourself in what you are trying to communicate regardless of the piano's strengths or weaknesses.'

One thing on which most performers agree is that it does get easier with experience. As Steven Isserlis says, 'My nerves have never really become less, but I comfort myself with the thought that I've been through all this hundreds of times. That usually makes me feel a bit better; if I didn't crack up last time (presuming that I didn't!), why should I this time?'

And your attitude to performance is crucial. Elvis Costello says, 'I carry with me two pieces of folk wisdom—nonsense things that take away the fear. The first is about a child who is climbing along a wall and thinks he's going to fall off. His father tells him, "You can't fall off because there's no one to stop you." While I'm pondering this, the fear has gone. The other is, "Never look up to a note, always look down." I've really taken that advice. If you think you're going to fail, you probably will.'

Practical tips for mind and body

For some, worrying about things in advance may help reduce anxiety. Various studies have shown that experienced players learn to let their anxiety peak just before the performance. For Steven Isserlis it's a question of balance: 'If I go on stage feeling too calm, then nerves can hit me as I start playing. If I have some nerves beforehand, there's a chance they will evaporate before I play.' Joanna MacGregor also believes in anticipating what might happen: 'I think a lot of people get really nervous when the cold reality of what they're doing hits them as they step out on stage. If you can get into the habit, in advance, of imagining yourself playing in this environment—whether it be a school hall or a classroom or a church—then whatever happens to you on the day, you will have slightly pre-empted.'

The importance of thorough practice is vital. As Steven Isserlis says, 'Feeling technically secure with a piece means that I can concentrate on listening to the music I'm playing.' Gillian Weir agrees: 'The single most important factor is to know the music. This sounds too basic to mention, but in fact most nervousness comes from a superficial knowledge of the piece. One must not still be "reading" the work, at any level, when the time for performance has arrived.'

Stephen Kovacevich has some practical advice: 'If you're nervous about a specific passage, it's very important in your preparations that you don't just practise the passage itself, but also the passage immediately before it as well. It's a bit like doing a high dive; you don't just jump, you take a few run-up steps to it. So in performance, as the passage is coming up, you are prepared for it.' He also believes in an idea for practising which the pianist and conductor Vladimir Ashkenazy taught him: 'Every so often say to yourself, "I'm going to play this piece from beginning to end, no matter what happens. If I mess up a passage I won't stop and practise it." If you stick to this, it does give you a sense of performing and coping with whatever happens. And if you can do this at home, it will help enormously when you get on stage.'

However, as the day of the concert arrives, over-practising can be far more of a danger than under-practising. Steven Isserlis says, 'I won't practise the piece I'm playing more than once on the day of the concert. After that I tend to play something else. So my fingers are keeping warm and working on intonation, but I'm not slaving away at the piece.'

This also applies to preparing your whole body for the performance. Joanna MacGregor says, 'What you eat and taking into account other factors in your life are terribly important. Not just on the day of a concert, but in the days leading up to it. I think you need to work backwards from a performance and start preparing for it quite a long way in advance. Really think carefully about late nights—it's no good starting to prepare your body on the day of a concert. It would be a bit like going on a crash diet on the day of a date—it's too late!'

Relaxation is crucial, even more important than last-minute practising. Steven Isserlis says, 'Being obsessive about the concert can be dangerous. I try to go out for a walk on the day of the concert and have as normal a day as I can.' Christian Lindberg has found that yoga really helps: 'Usually with wind and brass players it is the breath that is the first thing to go when you are nervous. I discovered yoga by accident when I had back problems. Your aim in yoga is to keep a steady breath even in the most difficult exercises. By training every day I discovered that I could keep breathing even in the most difficult circumstances and I thought, "Aha, this is really going to help with my nerves."' Joanna MacGregor believes that this kind of relaxation needs to be put in place well before the day of a performance: 'I think finding something that you enjoy doing that sets up a kind of meditative rhythm is a good idea. During performance your heartbeat quickens and your blood runs faster. You are in a state of alertness and often quite zingy. So if you can find something to counterbalance this, particularly in the days before, you can do a lot to get yourself ready.'

It is important to recognize your own foibles. Most musicians have an area that particularly bothers them. Having the right clothes is important for Elvis Costello: 'My wife says that when I do exhibit nerves I'll focus on some really weird thing that I would never notice otherwise, like my socks. I like to arrive at the theatre in the clothes I'm performing in. I don't like feeling I'm going to be rushed. I also carry a spare shirt or tie in case I drop something on it. No one is going to applaud you for the clothes you're wearing, but you have to feel right.'

Getting to know your own body's responses to nerves is vital for Joanna MacGregor: 'I noticed that I would get very sleepy and very tired before I had to perform and I'd get panic-struck about this. I would think, "This is terrible, this is terrible." What I've discovered is that this always happens to me and it's kind of like my body shutting down, making me have a little rest before I go on stage. Now it doesn't bother me and I think that's part of the key—not only do you begin to recognize the signals, you actually welcome them because they are mechanisms to help you prepare.'

It is also important to know where your fears lie. For Steven Isserlis it is memory lapses: 'I once had a memory lapse that was very bad; it didn't matter too much to anyone else, but it mattered a lot to me. Since then, I've slightly lost confidence in my memory.' Steven's solution is to work on a piece away from his instrument: 'I tend to play my part through on the piano, so that I know the memory is not just in my fingers.'

All musicians stress the importance of rest on the day of the concert. Steven Isserlis tries to structure the day of the concert so that he doesn't have to get up too early. 'If this is not possible or I haven't had a good night's sleep, I try to get a rest in the afternoon.' Elvis Costello warns singers about talking too much on the day of a concert: 'For most singers the telephone is a bad instrument. If you spend the afternoon talking on the telephone when you should have been resting, you are undermining your confidence. So try to avoid things like that.'

Try to find something that helps relax you in the last hour before the performance. I have heard about some unusual devices, ranging from a singer who hides behind the door of his dressing-room before the concert, to the violinist, Joshua Bell, who expends his nervous energy in making paper darts and then sets himself impossible tasks involving getting the darts into wastepaper bins in far corners of the room. Elvis Costello knows musicians who meditate, but for him a hot drink helps most of all.

He also advises on the importance of warming up: 'Don't forget to do your warm-ups. If you find there isn't anywhere suitable near the stage to warm up, be strong and ask someone to find you somewhere. But remember also to ask them to make sure you don't miss your cue. Find a routine, and stick to it, regardless of what anyone else says. After all, you are the performer.'

Even if you are not a wind or brass player or a singer, you need to practise deep breathing. A few breathing exercises before you go on stage can make all the difference. Christian Lindberg says, 'I take a deep breath in and when I blow out I point my hand out in front of me in a line with my nose. As I am breathing out, I am aiming the energy away from me and out to the audience. This gets me away from feeling introverted.'

Elvis Costello also warns singers about talking to anyone just before they go on stage: 'I don't think it's a good idea to have people in the green room beforehand, because it's very important to pitch your voice for what you are going to sing.

I speak an awful lot lower than I sing. So if I speak a lot before going on stage my voice becomes pitched in a totally different way.'

Many musicians have talked about the all-important moment as you walk on stage. And the advice is always this: before you go into the exam room or on to the stage, take two deep breaths and then smile as you start walking. You'll be amazed at the difference this makes.

It is also important to make eye contact with the examiner or audience. People become much less frightening when you actually see them. Why else are we so afraid of the dark? Remember that audiences are human beings too. As Elvis Costello and Gillian Weir point out, they are on your side, otherwise they wouldn't be there.

Before you go on stage take two
deep breaths and smile …

As well as breathing and relaxation exercises, Gillian Weir advocates visualization techniques: 'Imagine yourself playing well and *enjoying* what you are doing. Live in the moment. Too often we waste time, concentration and focus by regretting the past ("Whoops, was that a wrong note?") and fearing the future ("I hope I get through the awful bit on page 10") and not living in the present. The present is where all our faculties need to be so as to communicate the piece to the listener.'

Once on stage, Steven Isserlis stresses the importance of being aware of your whole body. As a string player it is easy to concentrate on tension in the arms or legs, but for Steven it is much more apparent in the face: 'If I see people playing with tension in the face or mouth, it's energy misdirected. Someone once told me that if your lips are slightly parted, you are less likely to be tense in the neck.' Think of who you are playing to. For Steven, a common trait of string players is to look at the finger board. When he coaches cellists, he gets them to look at an object on the other side of the room. 'It's amazing how much the sound changes. You need to be free of the instrument. Your shoulders will be more relaxed if your head is not craned forward, and if you're not looking down frantically you can listen to what the music is saying to you.'

Feel the atmosphere. Once you have started directing your energy out to the audience, it's important to be part of the atmosphere in the room or hall. For Christian Lindberg, this is crucial: 'I like to know how I'm going to feel before I play, so I go out on to the stage quite early so that I can feel the atmosphere.'

And finally, remember you are not necessarily the best judge of the performance. Even if you don't feel at your absolute best, you may still have given a wonderful performance. As Elvis Costello says, 'The number of times I've been told I've given the best concert of my life and I've felt it was the worst show I've ever done. In your efforts to sing around a vocal problem, you may have given more to the music than you realized and therefore touched people in a way you couldn't have done with a perfect throat. I don't really regard any of my recordings as definitive or unbeatable. I like the idea that I may perform any of my songs better any night. I might get something out of them that I didn't know was there.'

5 Whose performance is it anyway?

This book is primarily written for the performer, the person who has chosen to get up on stage or go into the exam room. But as with all things in life, everybody needs support from others when under pressure. My recommendations in this chapter are for those supporters—parents, friends, relations and teachers—who can give invaluable help in the days leading up to a performance or exam.

I talked to a number of parents and teachers to find out how best to support children and pupils. Their advice came in two forms: ideas on achieving a good general attitude towards the performer you are supporting; and ideas on how to give more practical support both psychologically and physically.

General support: your attitude is vital

Be aware that it is your child or pupil who needs to be interested in and focused on what they are doing, not you. Christine Brown, a highly experienced teacher in Leeds, believes this is crucial in tackling performance nerves: 'The aim should be to give pleasure to the listener. If the performers have this desire to communicate, it will prevent them from thinking about their own feelings of anxiety.'

Musical appreciation is not the same as technical ability. A child who shows great interest in music may not necessarily turn into the next child prodigy. Lin Marsh, an advisory music teacher in Oxfordshire, is much more interested in the enjoyment of performing: 'I'm interested in getting every child involved in wanting to give and communicate, to perform and enjoy music. I'm trying to get the very best out of children who may not have a great deal to give. Some parents are only looking for the best or better results than other people.'

Put yourself in the child's shoes. Try to remember what you felt at that age and how one little remark stayed with you, sometimes for years. Remember your own experiences and the effect of other people's expectations on you and try not to repeat the pattern. As Lin Marsh says, 'I think there shouldn't be any pressure from the parent, because there's enough pressure already. And it's the performance—either in the exam or in the hall—not the result that matters.'

Richard Crozier, Head of Professional Development at the Associated Board of the Royal Schools of Music, is very wary of pushing children too hard: 'Never push your child or pupil into doing the next exam or performing certain pieces before they are ready. As any parent knows, the speed of development varies enormously from child to child. Different people need differing amounts of time to absorb a piece of music technically and musically.'

Always check that your child or pupil wants to do, and is ready for, the impending performance. It's rarely too late to postpone an exam or performance. On the other hand, a positive attitude is vital. Christine Brown advises, 'Let your child or pupil know that you have faith in them and avoid last-minute instructions. Assume

A child who shows great interest in music may not necessarily turn into the next child prodigy …

31

that all will be well.' Be positive towards them in everything they do, not just when they are performing. Christine feels that it is particularly important after a performance to reassure them that you are still proud of them, regardless of what happened: 'Do not show annoyance or blame them, but offer assurance that you have faith in them and will help them prepare for the next performance.'

Performing music is the same whether it is in the sitting room or on a concert platform. Encourage your child to play for you and others as often as possible, so that the issue of 'performing' does not get out of proportion. Lin Marsh believes that teachers should always include performance as part of the lesson: 'If you're working with a child on a piece, before you end the lesson you can say, "I want you to perform that piece to me. I want you to come in, from that door, and I want you to take your place at the music stand, and I want you to play it to me, and I'm going to enjoy it. I don't care if you make mistakes. Till now we've been doing the learning and the practising, and now we're going to perform it." I think in practice regimes there should always be a time when it's a performance—even if it's only six bars.'

Try to turn the nerves your child or pupil may feel into a positive force. Feeling nervous can be exciting, and what they are about to do is exciting. Lin Marsh says, 'I always give them huge praise at the end. I would also point out if they scratched their nose in the middle of it, because you can't do that during a performance. I think they need to learn how to perform. It's different—it has a different feel about it.'

Be aware that pre-performance nerves are not only normal but can result in some apparently out-of-character behaviour. Christine Brown's advice in these circumstances is quite straightforward: 'Don't fuss! Keep to the normal routine and keep calm.'

Encourage your pupil or child to experience all sorts of musical activity by playing in orchestras and chamber groups, singing in choirs and listening to a variety of music. A trip to a live concert, particularly if it includes a piece by a composer they know, can be really stimulating. It may also give them a role model in the form of the calm soloist.

Pre-performance nerves can result in some out-of-character behaviour ...

Practical support

On top of the overall support you can give your child or pupil, there are many other ways in which you can help. What level of practical and psychological support you give depends very much on the needs of the person concerned, so be careful not to assume anything and always check with them that you are helping, not making the situation worse.

Christine Brown lists some classic signs of nerves: unsettled stomach, no desire to eat, yawning, shortness of breath and trembling. She advises parents and teachers to be on the lookout for them, but not to assume that they are automatically connected with performance nerves: 'Discuss it with the pupil or child. Try to find out if there is any particular reason.'

The strategy for helping your child or pupil depends very much on what kind of person they are: a 'right-brainer' (gestalt dominant) or a 'left-brainer' (logic dominant). Richard Crozier believes that this is fundamental to the way that children learn and behave. 'In very general terms, the logic dominant learner is likely to be more systematic in their practice and in the build-up to an exam or performance. A gestalt dominant learner may need more help in organizing themselves and will benefit from structured support. Remember, if the pupil does need some help in devising a practice schedule, be careful not to be over-zealous. A 'right-brainer' often does not need to be told that they are disorganized.'

Christine Brown believes that proper preparation is the best way to overcome nerves: 'No child should be asked to perform a piece unless they are confident of being able to play it well. Teacher, parents and child should have a positive attitude to the performance.'

Whether they are 'left-' or 'right-brainers', try to give as much of the responsibility for practice to your child or pupil as possible. Encourage them to work out a realistic timetable and stick to it. Also work out some form of reward system so that you can celebrate their achievements with them. This is important both for practice and for after an exam or performance, Lin Marsh says. 'If any of my children had an exam and I met them afterwards, I would reward them. We went for lunch or tea, and we had a good time. The results were immaterial. They were rewarded for all the work they had put in. We never gave them anything for achieving—we only encouraged the ongoing work.'

When it comes to practising, you cannot do it for them. What you can do is make sure the environment is right.

Richard Crozier recommends, 'Try to minimize the distractions around them as they practise. Get to know when is the best time of day for your child to practise and whether they benefit from one longer or several shorter practice sessions. Conversely don't make your child or pupil feel that they must hide away to practise. A feeling of isolation when practising only makes the performance situation feel even more strange and unnatural.'

Richard Crozier also thinks that sensitivity to problems as they occur is very important: 'Be aware that there may be a very good reason why your child or pupil is reluctant to practise a certain piece. If they find something hard, they do not want to hear themselves getting it wrong. Be gentle in helping them overcome their fears.'

If you are a teacher, give them a good model by your teaching. Demonstrate to them first hand that enjoyment and self-expression are more important than getting the notes right. This is far more powerful than merely talking about it.

Encourage your child or pupil to judge their own performance, but don't forget that any criticism needs to be constructive. Get them to say what they enjoyed about their playing. If your pupil or child invites your comments on their playing, you also need to make your criticism constructive. But be aware of making comparisons, as these can lead to feelings of inferiority. Lin Marsh advises, 'I think you have to give them lots of let-outs as to why it didn't go as they had hoped. It mustn't be, "I'm not good enough."'

Communication between parent and teacher is fundamentally important. As Lin Marsh says, 'In the build-up to an exam or a performance, parents should really be liaising with the teacher, and making sure the child is completely aware of everything that's going to happen in the exam. Sometimes examinees are not told that they might be stopped before the end of a piece. The parents have to know from the teacher everything that's likely to happen in that room. When I was preparing kids for exams, I used to wander around the room and bang a book down on the floor, and say, "This could happen, don't lose your focus."'

Richard Crozier believes that in the days leading up to, and on the day of, a performance your practical input can be so important in helping things to go smoothly—from what to wear and the planning of meals, to the actual business of being in the right place at the right time: 'Find out what your child is going to wear and get them to play in their concert clothes at least a week before. There is nothing worse than putting on "special" clothes and finding you can't breathe or lift your arms up. Experiment until they feel comfortable.' Getting the balance right between not eating at all and eating too much is also very important. 'Try to make sure they have eaten well in advance. Most people do not play at their best on a full stomach, but similarly an empty stomach can increase anxiety. If they really don't want to eat, make sure they have drunk plenty. Nerves cause us to sweat more (even in cold weather) and it's very easy to become dehydrated.'

Make sure that you know where the venue is and that you leave plenty of time to get there. Your confidence in this will encourage your child or pupil. If you are in a panic, it is no help at all. Leave enough time for them to acclimatize to the new environment. Their nerves will only increase if they arrive with cold hands or in a hot and bothered state.

Before and after the exam or performance, remind your child or pupil that the examiner and audience are on their side—and so are you. Show that you are proud of them and believe in them. Above all, allow them to express themselves—their fears and anxieties, as well as their triumph and joy.

Don't be surprised if there are tears immediately after an exam or performance. It is a perfectly normal way of releasing tension and you can help by being as calm and supportive as possible. Lin Marsh believes that your attitude after the performance is as important as it is in the build-up: 'If a performance has gone badly, just lighten up—it's not the end of the world. There will be other opportunities. It's not a big issue. We all have things which go badly. I just say, "Let's move on from there." I'm not a great one for post-mortems.'

Above all, remember that there are no rules and no certainties. Your child or pupil may not suffer from performance nerves at all; they may thrive on them. What is important is to let them be themselves. As Lin Marsh says, 'There are people whose nerves run for them, and people whose nerves seem to run more against them. I'm lucky because my nerves have always, so far, enhanced my performance. And it's the same with my three children. I don't know whether that's just luck, or the way we've approached it. Maybe we're all just extroverts and show-offs!'

6 How did I do?

You now have a whole range of strategies for coping with an attack of nerves. Some are practical and some a little more bizarre. Your parents, teachers and friends all have ideas on how to help support you and now the 'big day' has arrived. So what happens when you come off stage or out of the exam room?

Most professional performers will tell you that coping with performance nerves does get easier with experience. Everybody makes mistakes, and most people learn from them. Remember what you did when you first fell off your bike? You got back on again … and again … and again … until suddenly one day you could ride a bike. In Chapter 3 Elvis Costello urged you to remember that you are not always the best judge of your own performance. This chapter will give you ways of dealing with the inevitable post-mortem.

General preparation

The most important thing to understand is that in performance there is no 'pass' or 'fail'. One of the hardest things to do is to live up to an expectation. It's bad enough when these expectations are coming from those around you—knowing that someone else wants you to do well can add hugely to the tension. What can be even worse is your own (often impossibly high) expectations of yourself.

1. Have confidence in your own ability. This doesn't mean you won't feel nervous, but it does mean that after the event you can believe that you did your best under the circumstances.

2. It is human nature to remember less positive elements at the expense of the positive. So try to think about the successes you've had in the past (and not just in music) and try to visualize yourself having done well. If you start to think about how badly the performance went, it can become a self-fulfilling prophecy the next time.

3. Try not to be cross with yourself for having felt nervous. Remind yourself that the symptoms of nerves—sweating, thumping heart, shortness of breath, shaking limbs—are quite normal.

4. Try to remember that the audience probably didn't notice that you were nervous. When you are nervous the body produces adrenalin and whether you are a musician or an athlete you cannot perform at your best without it. Adrenalin is the fuel that gives your performance a certain edge which the audience will have enjoyed.

5. A musical performance is not just about technical perfection, so if you did make a mistake or two you won't have ruined the whole performance. Part of the thrill of live performance is the element of risk. It is also partly what stimulates the audience. Think about your own experience of listening to a live TV or radio broadcast. If the presenter makes a mistake, it can add to the power of the broadcast—it makes it more real.

6. Nervous tension can be positive if it finds expression in the intensity of the performance. As the performer you are not the best person to evaluate this. Try to think back to the audience's reaction. They probably didn't hear any of those 'mistakes' you are so painfully remembering. They were applauding because they actually enjoyed what you played.

7. Nerves affect everyone, even the professionals. But what the professionals recognize is that it does get easier with experience. Each crisis you deal with in a positive way will help you cope better with the next.

Prepare to relax: mind and body

In Chapter 1 we saw how the word tension means 'stretching', and how this tension must be balanced by relaxation. So when you first come off the stage (or out of the exam room), take a few moments to breathe deeply and relax all those tense muscles.

1. Try to look forward to relaxing after all that build-up. Plan to do something you really enjoy immediately after the performance. And make it something where you will have little time to over-analyse what happened. There'll be plenty of time for that later!
2. Put things in context. Try to imagine the worst thing that could have happened. Isn't this worse than the possibility that you made a few mistakes?
3. Think about why you went on stage in the first place. What you have just done is about far more than living up to expectations. Also try to think about your own personal enjoyment and not the audience's. See if you can find a passage or a moment that you really enjoyed and savour that memory.
4. Don't be too hard on yourself, and try to see a less than perfect performance as part of learning to be a musician. Remember that it does get easier with experience.
5. It's also worth remembering that one of the most precious things about live performance is that it can never be

Don't be too hard on yourself …

repeated. This also applies if you feel you did very badly. You will never do it badly like that again!

6. Think about yourself as a listener. During a performance most listeners will not be able to spot a couple of wrong notes or an altered rhythm because music happens in real time. Once the sound has gone past, you don't think, 'Was that right?' because you are busy listening to the next bit.

7. If you really did feel that things went very badly, look at whether you pushed yourself too far by playing something that you weren't quite ready for. Talk about the choice of pieces with your teacher.

8. Let your family, friends or teacher know how you feel after the event. If someone has said something that's upset you, tell them, otherwise they may have no idea that what was intended as a helpful hint has made you feel worse.

9. If this wasn't a solo performance, try to be positive and constructive in your feedback, both to your fellow musicians and to yourself. Talk through what happened with them and try to listen to their positive remarks as well as the criticism.

10. Enjoy the feeling of a shared musical experience. This is one of the most wonderful things about music. Do something together, particularly something that will help release tension—a good laugh can work wonders.

11. Although you may not always be the best judge of how well or how badly the performance went, if you do feel good about it (even if it was for just a few bars) relish the feeling. Part of the compensation for all those pre-performance nerves is the post-performance euphoria. So don't let anyone or anything stop you enjoying it!

So we've got a few things straight: performance nerves are normal, most people suffer from them in some form, they can be deeply unpleasant, but they do get better with experience—or at least we can become better at coping with them. One question still remains. Why do we put ourselves through all this misery? Answer: because making music is fun. It's rewarding, it's stimulating, it's part of life and it's what we have chosen to do. And, as we have seen, nerves can also be useful and give our performance an edge; in fact, in some ways they are vital to the essence of performing.

In this final chapter I will try to pull together some of the ideas we have looked at about the sources of performance nerves and learning how to deal with them, even turning those nerves to our advantage. Much of this can be done by understanding why we have decided to make music or become performers, ensuring that we have put ourselves in this potentially stressful situation for the right reasons.

General preparation for enjoying yourself

It is important to understand that the ideas in this book are not a prescription for curing performance nerves, they are only suggestions. It is not a simple matter of saying, 'Oh, I feel nervous therefore I will do x, y or z', it is much more about understanding what it is that makes us feel nervous and how we might help ourselves.

1. Appreciating the importance of what you are doing is a good step. Music plays an important part in most people's lives. When people are asked to list their hobbies or

interests, most will include music or some kind of musical enthusiasm. How music affects each individual is almost impossible to monitor, but it does have an impact. You as the performer have the power to affect people in many different ways. This is something special and something you can be proud of.

2. Be convincing in what you do. Music is about sound, it's not about notation. As musicians we often get so worried about the notes on the page that we forget that what the listener wants to hear is the music. If you play a few wrong notes, it doesn't matter. What does matter is that what you play is convincing and real.

3. Music can be a way of expressing yourself. The German philosopher Ernst Bloch had a favourite saying: 'When we listen to music, what we hear is ourselves.' Music is something that comes from the inside, not something from the outside going in. Whatever you play will be in some way an expression of who you are. It's not about doing what your teacher tells you, it is about finding a way of saying what you want to say through music.

4. Remember why you are playing a musical instrument. Don't let other people's expectations create any extra tension. You are doing this for *you*.

5. Try to smile and look as if you're enjoying yourself. Remember that if the audience—be they friends, family, colleagues, teachers or examiners—sees that you are enjoying yourself, they will believe in you and the music you are playing.

Practical preparation

1. Make sure that before you consider performing a piece you are happy with this choice of music. Explore all the available options for changing your programme if you're not happy with it.

2. Plan carefully the order in which you are going to play your pieces. If you are prone to feeling nervous, start with a piece you know really well, or one that is not too technically demanding.

3. If you are playing with other people, it is vital that you get on, not just personally but musically. If possible try playing with lots of different people. Experiment with different accompanists, duo partners or ensembles. It can also be a great way to make new friends.

4. Remember the old cliché, 'All work and no play makes Jack a dull boy.' Make sure you have other interests and ways of relaxing. If you immerse yourself in music to the exclusion of everything else, you may be missing out on whole areas of experience that could enhance your playing.

5. Try to make practising fun too. It doesn't have to be a grind, you can do all sorts of silly things. Depending on what instrument you play (tubas and

double-basses do have some limitations), you can practise in the garden or the bath, on the kitchen table or sitting in the middle of a field or park. You can also practise with friends.

6. Play around with finding the different sounds your instrument can make. Try practising using different rhythms, playing something ridiculously fast or slow, happily or sadly, or using different articulation. Not only will this make practice more enjoyable, it may also help you decide how *you* want to play a particular piece or phrase.

7. Practising in front of a mirror can also be great fun. You will discover the difference in the sound you make depending on how you are feeling. Try playing while frowning, laughing, growling or smiling. Your mood affects not only the sound but how the audience might feel.

8. Whenever you are asked to play for someone, whether it's your teacher, your family or an audience of strangers, try to think of it as playing to them, not performing for them. Say to yourself, 'I'm going to enjoy playing this piece. The people listening want to hear me and I'm happy to play it. I'm going to do my best and if I do something wrong, it's just one of those things.'

9. How many times have you been to a concert or listened to a recording and come away thinking, 'Yes, that was good, but there was something missing?' A technically brilliant performance can be impressive and exciting, but unless there is feeling, intensity and musicality, the performance is just that—a performance—and not a musical experience.

10. Be enthusiastic and enjoy your music-making. If you really love the music and love playing your instrument, if you have practised hard and feel that what you play is part of you, not only will you give enormous pleasure to those listening, you might even have fun yourself!

This book is not about finding ways to get rid of your performance nerves, it's all about keeping your nerve and using it to your advantage. Good luck and, above all, enjoy making music!

Is there anything we could have done better? _____
_____
_____
_____

About you...

Name (*Mr/Mrs/Ms*) _____
Address _____
_____
_____ Postcode _____
Daytime tel nos _____
Email _____

Please only give us your mobile phone number or email if you wish to hear from us about other products and services from the AA and partners by text or mms, or email.

Which age group are you in?
Under 25 ☐   25–34 ☐   35–44 ☐   45–54 ☐   55–64 ☐   65+ ☐

How many trips do you make a year?
Less than one ☐   One ☐   Two ☐   Three or more ☐

Are you an AA member? Yes ☐   No ☐

About your trip...

When did you book? m m / y y   When did you travel? m m / y y

How long did you stay? _____

Was it for business or leisure? _____

Did you buy any other travel guides for your trip? _____

If yes, which ones? _____

Dear Reader

Your comments, opinions and recommendations are very important to us. Please help us to improve our travel guides by taking a few minutes to complete this simple questionnaire.

You do not need a stamp (unless posted outside the UK). If you do not want to cut this page from your guide, then photocopy it or write your answers on a plain sheet of paper.

Send to: **The Editor, AA World Travel Guides,
FREEPOST SCE 4598, Basingstoke RG21 4GY.**

Your recommendations...

We always encourage readers' recommendations for restaurants, nightlife or shopping – if your recommendation is used in the next edition of the guide, we will send you a **FREE AA Guide** of your choice from this series. Please state below the establishment name, location and your reasons for recommending it.

_____
_____
_____
_____
_____
_____

Please send me **AA Guide** _____

About this guide...
Which title did you buy?
    AA _____
Where did you buy it? _____
When? m m / y y
Why did you choose this guide?_____
_____
_____
_____
_____

Did this guide meet your expectations?
Exceeded ☐   Met all ☐   Met most ☐   Fell below ☐
Were there any aspects of this guide that you particularly liked? _____
_____
_____
_____

continued on next page...

Vancouver street index

Victoria street index

About this book

This book is divided into five sections.

The essence of Vancouver and the Canadian Rockies pages 6–19
Introduction; Features; Food and drink; Short break including the 10 Essentials

Planning pages 20–33
Before you go; Getting there; Getting around; Being there

Best places to see pages 34–55
The unmissable highlights of any visit to Vancouver and the Canadian Rockies

Best things to do pages 56–73
Great views; hiking and biking; places to take the children and more

Exploring pages 74–185
The best places to visit in Vancouver and the Canadian Rockies, organized by area

💎 to 💎💎💎💎 denotes AAA rating

Maps
All map references are to the maps on the covers. For example, Calgary has the reference ➕ 24G – indicating the grid square in which it is to be found

Admission prices
Inexpensive (under $7.50)
Moderate ($7.50–$15)
Expensive (over $15)

Hotel prices
Prices are per double room per night:
$ budget (under $150)
$$ moderate ($150–$250)
$$$ expensive to luxury (over $250)

Restaurant prices
Prices are for a three-course meal per person without drinks:
$ budget (under $25)
$$ moderate ($25–$45)
$$$ expensive (over $45)

Contents

BEST THINGS TO DO

EXPLORING...

56 – 73   74 – 185

The essence of...

Vancouver is one of the world's most beautiful cities, a glittering, modern metropolis fringed by the ocean and framed by forest-swathed mountains. Beyond its parks, beaches and shimmering skyscrapers, in the great wilderness of British Columbia, lies one of the world's most beautiful regions, a seemingly unending succession of lakes, waterfalls, forests and snow-covered peaks. Here are wolves, bears, eagles and other wildlife, as well as endless opportunities for hiking, skiing and other outdoor activities. This peerless domain reaches its climax in the majesty of the Canadian Rockies, protected by some of the most spectacular national parks on earth.

features

Vancouver is a beautiful city, but its beauty is more than skin deep. Walk around the pristine streets of its downtown core – the heart of a city that barely 150 years ago was merely a clearing in the forest – and you quickly realize there's more to this west coast metropolis than the great outdoors. Modern and dynamic, it is a place bolstered by a booming port, thriving movie business, youthful population and the thrill of having been awarded the 2010 Winter Olympic Games. It is also laid-back; a cultural and hedonistic hotspot blessed with fine museums, cutting-edge contemporary arts, rich nightlife, excellent shopping, and cafés and restaurants that are on a par with anything in New York or San Francisco.

In the wilds of British Columbia and the Rockies the story is a little different. This is a region of few towns and long distances, but also of some of the most scenic roads and spectacular landscapes imaginable. Many visitors concentrate on the parks of the Rockies, notably Banff and Jasper, but almost every corner of the region has its rewards, whether it's the mild-weathered lakes and vineyards of the Okanagan, the homey little villages of the Kootenays, or the crashing white-water torrents of the Fraser Canyon.

GEOGRAPHY
● Position of Vancouver: 49:15:00N 123:07:15W
● Size: 114.67sq km (44.26sq miles)

● Highest point in the Rockies:
Mount Robson, 3,954m (12,972ft)

CLIMATE
● Average Vancouver January
temperature: 5°C (41°F)
● Average Vancouver July
temperature: 23°C (73°F)
● Rainy days in January: 20
● Rainy days in July: 6
● Average January rainfall: 13.9cm
(5.5in)
● Average July rainfall: 3.6cm (1.4in)

TOURISM
● 8.9 million overnight visitors
annually
● 1 million cruise-ship visitors
annually
● Tourism worth $4.5 billion annually

PEOPLE
● Population 587,000 (2006)
● Greater Vancouver 2,116,581
● Canada's third-largest city

food & drink

Food is one of the great pleasures of a visit to Vancouver, thanks partly to the rich bounty of land and sea, which provide a superb array of locally sourced ingredients, and partly to its restaurants' wide range of cuisines, the legacy of the city's rich, multiethnic population.

There's no better place to appreciate the variety of ingredients available to Vancouver's chefs than Granville Island, home to one of North America's finest food markets. Among the cascades of fresh fruit and vegetables are stalls selling the world's best wild salmon and other sublime seafood, along with Albertan beef – again, some of the world's best – and a vast variety of other produce, much of it organic and seasonal. The picture is repeated across the city, and in British Columbia beyond, where eating out is every bit as important as in Vancouver.

CUISINES

If Vancouver is lucky in its natural ingredients, then it is luckier still in the wide variety of its cuisines. This is due largely to its position on the so-called Pacific Rim, a situation that has seen it absorb both the immigrants and the culinary influences of China, Japan, Vietnam, Cambodia, Korea and other countries. Almost anywhere you go in the city, you'll be able to enjoy – among much else – Chinese dim sum, Japanese noodles or Vietnamese soups, not forgetting French, Italian and many other Old World cuisines.

Across the city and beyond you'll also often find a cuisine variously described as fusion, West Coast or Pacific Rim, an inspired mixture of Asian, Italian and other influences that usually produces light, healthy and often innovative dishes full of flavor and variety. You'll also find classic North American food – great burgers, ribs, chicken wings and the like – often in excellent small chains such as Earls, Milestones or White Spot.

THE ESSENCE OF VANCOUVER & CANADIAN ROCKIES

EATING OUT

Vancouver has in excess of 4,000 restaurants, more per head of population than anywhere else in Canada. In some of these you may want to dress up, but on the whole, dining out in the city is relaxed and informal. This is especially true in the summer, when many restaurants open outdoor terraces (or decks), often with wonderful views. Prices are generally lower than in Europe, and portions generous. But good food doesn't stop in Vancouver's restaurants, for the city has a vibrant café culture, as well as plenty of inexpensive pubs, bars and lounges, which always sell food.

14

WINE

The days when Canadian wine was a joke are long gone, and many restaurants offer excellent wine, much of it produced virtually on Vancouver's doorstep, either on Vancouver Island or the Fraser Valley, or in the Okanagan region in central southern British Columbia. If you like the rounded, full-bodied and fruit-filled wines of California, Australia and New Zealand, then you'll enjoy the wines of Mission Hill, Sumac Ridge and other top Canadian producers. And if you don't want to risk a bottle, then most restaurants have plenty of wines by the glass.

short break

If you have only a short time to visit Vancouver and the Canadian Rockies and would like to take home some unforgettable memories, then do something that really captures the flavor of the city and the region beyond. The following suggestions will give you a wide range of sights and experiences that won't take long, won't cost too much, and will help make your visit special.

● **Ride the SeaBus.** Take the ferry (➤ 90) across the Burrard Inlet from Waterfront Station in downtown to North Vancouver to enjoy superb views of the port and city skyline.

● **Explore Stanley Park.** North America's largest city park is one of Vancouver's highlights, and its beaches, gardens, shady nooks and areas of untamed forest are easily seen on foot or by bicycle (➤ 54–55).

● **Eat in Chinatown.** Vancouver's Chinatown (➤ 80–81) is one of the largest and most authentic in the world, and dining here with local families lets you step instantly into another culture.

● **Visit Granville Island.** There's nowhere better in Vancouver to idle away a morning, to people-watch or to shop. The public market

(➤ 40–41) in particular is superb and there are dozens of galleries, artisans' workshops and small specialist stores.

● **Watch the sunset.** There are plenty of viewpoints or bars and restaurants where you can watch the sun go down in this most beautiful of cities. Or simply sit on the beaches on English Bay (➤ 83) or in Stanley Park (➤ 54–55).

● **Visit Grouse Mountain.** Ride North America's largest cable car up Grouse Mountain for the finest views in the city (➤ 42–43).

● **See the Royal BC Museum.** British Columbia is full of museums, large and small, that explore the region's social and natural history – this the best (➤ 52–53).

● **Drive the Icefields Parkway.** This is the one road to drive if you drive no other, a glorious highway that runs through some of the Canadian Rockies' best scenery (➤ 44–45).

● **Take at least one hike** – it doesn't have to be tough – it could be in one of Vancouver's parks or along one of the trails in Banff National Park (▶ 160–163) – but at some point you should sample the region's great outdoors at first hand.

● **Stop off in Kaslo and Nelson** – if two places encapsulate the small-town charm of British Columbia, and the Kootenays in particular, it is these two gems (▶ 46–47, 144–145), both beautifully situated and both full of historic houses, galleries, specialist shops, cafés and pretty streets.

Planning

Before you go

WHEN TO GO

JAN	FEB	MAR	APR	MAY	JUN	JUL	AUG	SEP	OCT	NOV	DEC
5°C	7°C	10°C	19°C	18°C	21°C	23°C	23°C	18°C	14°C	9°C	6°C
41°F	44°F	50°F	66°F	64°F	69°F	73°F	73°F	64°F	57°F	48°F	43°F

🔴 High season   ⬤ Low season

Temperatures are the average daily maximum for each month. The best time to visit Vancouver is June to August, when you can expect warm, sunny weather. The good weather often extends into September and October, when the city will also be less crowded and hotel prices lower. The same applies to much of interior British Columbia, though here conditions and temperatures can be more extreme and rainfall is generally lower. Snow is more prolonged, and cold more intense in mountainous areas, though the Okanagan region is an exception, with mild winters and hot, dry summers. In Calgary and the Rockies, snow can close roads for many months and persist on upland trails as late as June. Generally, July and August are warm fine months, and good, if popular, times to visit.

WHAT YOU NEED

- ● Required
- ○ Suggested
- ▲ Not required

Some countries require a passport to remain valid for a minimum period (usually at least six months) beyond the date of entry – check before you travel.

	UK	Germany	USA	Australia	Ireland	Netherlands	Spain
Passport (or National Identity Card where applicable)	●	●	●	●	●	●	●
Visa (regulations can change – check before you travel)	▲	▲	▲	▲	▲	▲	▲
Onward or Round-trip Ticket	●	●	▲	●	●	●	●
Health Inoculations (tetanus and polio)	▲	▲	▲	▲	▲	▲	▲
Health Documentation (► 23, Health Insurance)	○	○	○	○	○	○	○
Travel Insurance	○	○	○	○	○	○	○
Driving License (National)	●	●	●	●	●	●	●
Car Insurance Certificate	▲	▲	●	▲	▲	▲	▲
Car Registration Document	▲	▲	●	▲	▲	▲	▲

WEBSITES

www.tourismvancouver.com
www.tourismvictoria.com
www.hellobc.com

www.travelalberta.com
www.pc.gc.ca (National Parks)
www.canada.com

TOURIST OFFICES AT HOME

In the UK

PO Box 101, Chard,
Somerset, TA20 9AR
☎ 0870 380 0070
www.canada.travel

In the USA

www.canada.travel
(There is no phone or postal
contact/office for the general
public.)

HEALTH INSURANCE

Canada has excellent health provisions, but foreign visitors are required to pay for treatment, so it is essential that you take out health and travel insurance that will cover all potential costs, including the price of an emergency flight home. The EHIC (European Health Insurance Card) does not cover EU nationals for treatment in Canada. Keep all bills and receipts to make a claim.

Dental care is also excellent but costly, so include this in your insurance. Most hotels can recommend a dentist, or try the tourist office or Yellow Pages. Again, keep all documentation for your claim.

TIME DIFFERENCES

| GMT | Vancouver | Germany | USA (NY) | Netherlands | Spain |
| 12 noon | 4AM | 1PM | 7AM | 1PM | 1PM |

Vancouver and much of British Columbia are on Pacific Time, eight hours behind GMT (GMT-8). Calgary, Alberta and part of southeast British Columbia observe Mountain Standard Time (GMT-7). Daylight saving applies between April and October.

NATIONAL HOLIDAYS

Jan 1 *New Year's Day*
3rd Mon of Feb *Family Day* (Alberta)
Mar/Apr *Good Friday and Easter Monday*
3rd Mon in May *Victoria Day*
Jul 1 *Canada Day*
1st Mon in Aug *BC Day* (British Columbia)

1st Mon in Aug *Heritage Day* (Alberta)
1st Mon in Sep *Labour Day*
2nd Mon in Oct *Thanksgiving*
Nov 11 *Remembrance Day*
Dec 25 *Christmas Day*
Dec 26 *Boxing Day*

Banks, schools and government offices close on public holidays and many visitor attractions and transportation services follow Sunday openings and timetables. Holidays falling on a weekend are usually taken on the following Monday.

WHAT'S ON WHEN

The venues and events listed here are liable to change from one year to the next, and in the case of major festivals there is often more than one venue. Dates also vary slightly from year to year.

January *Chinese New Year:* 15 days of festivities (precise dates vary each year) in Vancouver's Chinatown and elsewhere. *Banff and Lake Louise Festival:* ski races, ice-sculpture competitions and skating parties.

February *Boat Show:* western Canada's largest and oldest boat show is held in Vancouver's BC Stadium over five days at the start of the month.

May *Vancouver Marathon* (first Sun in month): Canada's largest marathon attracts more than 6,000 runners (www.bmovanmarathon.ca). *International Children's Festival* (end of

May–early Jun): a week of events in Vancouver's Vanier Park attracts 70,000 people (www.childrensfestival.com).

June *Banff Festival:* large festival of the visual and performing arts.
Bard on the Beach (Jun–Sep): Shakespeare plays performed in outdoor venues in Vancouver (www.bardonthebeach.org).
Jazz Festival (10 days at end of month): more than 800 jazz and blues musicians perform at 25 venues around Vancouver (www.coastaljazz.ca).

July *Calgary Stampede:* one of the world's biggest and best rodeos.
Canada Day (Jul 1): celebrations across the region.
Folk Festival (3rd weekend of month): 30,000 people on Vancouver's Jericho Beach Park watch more than 100 different performers.
Celebration of Light (dates vary): the world's largest fireworks competition attracts 500,000 people to Vancouver's English Bay over four nights.

August *Abbotsford Air Show:* one of the world's best air shows takes place 58km (36 miles) from Vancouver (www.abbotsfordairshow.com).
Pride Parade: colorful parade and events celebrating Vancouver's gay and lesbian community (www.vancouverpride.ca).

September *Fringe Theatre Festival* (10–14 days mid-month): theater, comedy and dance groups perform more than 500 shows at venues around Vancouver.
Vancouver Film Festival (17 days): North America's third-largest film festival presents more than 500 screenings of films new and old (www.viff.org).

October *Wine festivals:* events and tastings held across the Okanagan region to celebrate the wine harvest.

November *VanDusen Market and Festival of Light* (late Nov–Dec): gift and craft market in Vancouver's VanDusen garden, which is illuminated with 20,000 lights.

December *Christmas Carol Ship Parade* (3 weeks to Christmas): magical flotillas of illuminated boats with carol singers in Vancouver's harbor.

Getting there

BY AIR

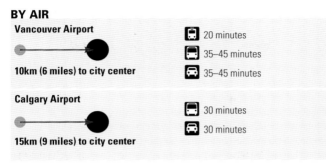

Vancouver Airport

10km (6 miles) to city center

🚇 20 minutes

🚌 35–45 minutes

🚗 35–45 minutes

Calgary Airport

15km (9 miles) to city center

🚌 30 minutes

🚗 30 minutes

The main entry to Vancouver and western British Columbia is Vancouver International Airport (tel: 604/207-7077; www.yvr.ca). SkyTrain (tel: 604/953-3333; www.translink.bc.ca), the city's light-transit system (➤ 28), runs from the airport to Waterfront Station near Canada Place. Alternatively, take the Airporter shuttle bus (tel: 604/946-8866 or 1-800/668-3141; www.yvrairporter.com) from outside the International Arrivals terminal (every 20–30 minutes from 5:20am–11:45pm).

For Banff, Calgary and the Canadian Rockies, Calgary Airport (tel: 403/735-1200 or 1-877/254-7427; www.calgaryairport.com) is a more convenient entry point.

BY TRAIN

Vancouver is served by VIA Rail (tel: 1-888/842-7245; www.viarail.com) services from Kamloops, Jasper and points in eastern Canada, plus Amtrak (tel: 1-800/872-7245; www.amtrak.com) services from Eugene, Portland and Seattle. Trains arrive at the Pacific Central Station alongside the bus terminal (➤ 27). Calgary has no public train service, but is served by occasional expensive private charter trains.

BY CAR

From eastern Canada or central US, the main Trans-Canada Highway (Hwy 1) runs through the heart of British Columbia to Vancouver via

Calgary, Banff and Kamloops. Hwy 3 is a slower trans-provincial route in the south shadowing the US border; Hwy 6 is a still slower but scenic route through the center of the province. Hwy 5 and Hwy 16 form another scenic road, linking Vancouver and Jasper.

BY BUS

Greyhound (tel: 1-800/661-8747; www.greyhound.ca) offers a network of services across most of Canada, including several services daily between Calgary and Vancouver and many points in between, including Banff and Lake Louise. From Vancouver's main bus terminal (1150 Station Street) take a taxi to downtown for around $7–$10 or the SkyTrain service to Waterfront Station from Science World-Main Street station, 150m (165yds) from the terminal.

Getting around

PUBLIC TRANSPORTATION

Internal flights Air Canada (www.aircanada.ca), plus smaller regional airlines, including seaplane operators such as Harbour Air (tel: 604/274-1277; www.harbour-air.com) in Vancouver, provide regular services between Vancouver, Calgary, Victoria and Edmonton, plus the Gulf Islands and many other smaller centers in British Columbia.

Trains Railway services are limited. VIA Rail (tel: 1-888/842-7245; www.viarail.com) has three services weekly between Vancouver and eastern Canada via Kamloops, Jasper and Edmonton, plus services from Victoria to Courtenay on Vancouver Island and from Jasper to Prince George and Prince George to Prince Rupert.

Regional buses Greyhound (tel: 1-800/661-8747; www.greyhound.ca) provides the majority of regional bus services. Key smaller operators include Pacific Coach Lines (tel: 604/662-7575 or 1-800/661-1725; www.pacificcoach.com) for services from Vancouver to Victoria, inclusive of ferry crossing, and Perimeter (tel: 604/266-5386 or 1-877/317-7788; www.perimeterbus.com) for departures to Whistler.

Ferries Victoria has ferry connections to Seattle and to various other points on the US west coast. BC Ferries (tel: 250/386-3431; www.bcferries.com) offers ferries from Vancouver to Victoria and other towns on Vancouver Island, plus the Gulf Islands. It also runs ferries from Port Hardy on Vancouver Island to Prince Rupert. Vancouver is a major port for cruise ships (► 11).

Urban transportation Translink (tel: 604/953-3333; www.translink.bc.ca) operates Vancouver's public transportation (or transit) system, which includes buses, the SeaBus to North Vancouver, and SkyTrain, a light-rail network. Tickets and day passes should be bought before traveling at authorized outlets or ticket vending machines. The tickets are then valid across all three services for 90 minutes from the moment they are validated.

TAXIS

Vancouver taxis are inexpensive and efficient. If you can't find a cab on the street, head for the big hotels, where taxis tend to congregate. Alternatively, call a cab from Black Top & Checker (tel: 604/731-1111), Maclure's (tel: 604/683-6666) or Vancouver Taxi (tel: 604/871-1111).

DRIVING

- In Canada, you drive on the right and pass on the left.
- All persons in a car must wear seat belts.
- Right turns are allowed at red lights, after coming to a full stop, unless otherwise indicated.
- Distances and speed limits are given in kilometers and kilometers per hour. Speed limits vary between provinces, but are generally 100kph (62mph) on expressways, 70–90kph (43–56mph) on other major roads, and 50kph (31mph) or less in urban areas.
- Fuel (gas) is sold by the liter. Fill up when you can in mountain areas, where fuel stops may be few and far between.
- Most roads are of high quality, but some mountain roads may be surfaced with gravel rather than asphalt.
- If you intend to drive long distances, consider joining the Canadian Automobile Association (www.caa.ca).
- In case of emergency, call 911.

CAR RENTAL

Car rental is available at airports, cities and resorts, as well as many towns. Rates depend on location. You must be over 21 to rent a car, and have ID and a valid driver's license, which you have held for at least a year. If crossing between Alberta and British Columbia, check that the rental agreement allows you to take the car into another province. Also check for penalties when dropping a car in a different place to where it was rented. If you rent in the US, carry a copy of the rental agreement. Rental companies often do not allow cars to be taken on gravel roads.

FARES AND CONCESSIONS

Children and students in possession of valid student ID, plus seniors, often qualify for reductions on public transportation and many attractions in Vancouver and across British Columbia and the Canadian Rockies.

Being there

TOURIST OFFICES

● Vancouver
TouristInfo Centre, 200 Burrard Street ☎ 604/683-2000; www.tourismvancouver.com

● Victoria
812 Wharf Street ☎ 250/953-2033; www.tourismvictoria.com

● Banff
224 Banff Avenue ☎ 403/762-1550; www.pc.gc.ca or www.banfflakelouise.com

● Calgary
Calgary Tower, 101 9th Avenue SW ☎ 403/750-2362; www.tourismcalgary.com

● Jasper
500 Connaught Drive ☎ 780/852-6176; www.pc.gc.ca

● Lake Louise
Lake Louise Village ☎ 403/522-3833; www.pc.gc.ca or www.banfflakelouise.com

MONEY

A Canadian dollar is made up of 100 cents. The one cent piece, or penny, is copper in color. There are also five-cent pieces (nickels), ten cents (dimes) and 25 cents (quarters). The gold-colored one-dollar piece is known as a "loonie." The two-dollar piece, or "toonie," is silver and gold. Notes (bills) come in denominations of $5 (blue), $10 (purple), $20 (green), $50 (pink) and $100 (brown). There have been counterfeit problems with $50 and $100 notes. New designs for $5, $10 and $20 notes have been introduced, but old designs remain legal tender.

All major credit cards are accepted and there are ATMs, banks and other exchange facilities. UK and European visitors should check with their bank about withdrawing cash from ATMs.

TIPS/GRATUITIES

Yes ✓ No ✗		
Hotels (if service included)	✓	change
Restaurants (if service not included)	✓	15–20%
Cafés/bars (if service not included)	✓	change
Taxis	✓	change
Tour guides	✓	$1
Porters/chambermaids	✓	$1
Toilet attendants	✗	

POSTAL AND INTERNET SERVICES

Stamps can be bought from post offices and outlets with post office facilities (look for blue-and-red window signs), notably convenience stores such as 7-Eleven and Shopper's Drug Mart. Vancouver's main post office is 349 West Georgia Street at Homer Street, tel: 604/662-5723; www. canadapost.ca, open Mon–Fri 8–5:30. There are plans under way to relocate it.

The internet is accessible across Canada, with many cybercafés in towns and cities and WiFi and broadband connections in many hotels. However, access is often restricted in mountain and other rural areas.

TELEPHONES
Emergency telephone numbers
Police, fire, ambulance and general emergencies ☎ 911
Outgoing calls
To call abroad the prefix is 011, then the country code: for the UK dial 011 44 then the number minus the "0" at the start of the area code. For Australia the country code is 61, New Zealand 64 and the Republic of Ireland 353.
Calls to the US
It is easy to make calls directly to the US from Canada. Dial 1 followed by the state or city code, then the telephone number.
Incoming calls
To call Vancouver from the UK and the rest of Europe, dial 001 and then the number, including the 604 prefix. The 604 prefix must always be dialed, even when calling 604 numbers within Vancouver itself.
Regional phone codes
The code for Victoria and most of interior British Columbia is 250. Calgary and parts of the Rockies have a 403 code. In Jasper and northern British Columbia the code is 867.
Calls from hotels
You often pay a high tariff to use direct-dial services from hotel rooms. However, many Vancouver hotels offer free local calls (604 numbers within the city).
Mobile (cell) phones
Contact your service provider to check whether your handset will work on Canada's 1900 megaHerz network.

Pay phones
Use ¢25 coins and/or credit cards. Dial "0" for an operator, "00" for the international operator. For directory enquiries, call 411: the cost is ¢75.

CUSTOMS REGULATIONS
Adults over 19 can bring 1.14L of wine or spirits, 8.5L of beer, 200 cigarettes, 50 cigars and 200g of tobacco into the country. Also allowed are gifts up to a value of $65 and a "reasonable" amount of goods such as computers and outdoor equipment for personal use. Firearms are prohibited, as are meat, fish, fruit, vegetables and plants. Contact the Canada Customs and Revenue Agency (tel: 204/983 3500 or 1-800/461-9999; www.ccra-adrc.gc.ca/visitors) for more information.

METRIC MEASUREMENTS
Canada uses the metric system of weights and measures: centimeters, meters and kilometers for distance, grams and kilograms for weight, liters for fuel.

OPENING HOURS

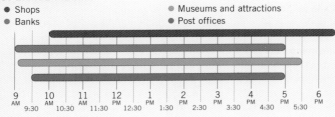

Shops: Vary considerably. Most city shops, especially those in busy or tourist areas, open daily in summer 10–8 or later; otherwise Mon–Sat 10–5. Convenience stores have longer hours, often 24 hours daily.
Banks: Most banks open Mon–Fri 9 or 9:30–5, though some may open from 8–8 plus shorter hours on Sat, but close Mon.
Museums and attractions: Vary considerably. Many have shorter hours from Labour Day (first Mon in Sep) to Victoria Day (third Mon in May).
Post offices: Generally Mon–Fri 9:30–5, sometimes Sat 10–4 or similar, but outlets in convenience stores have longer hours.

ELECTRICITY

Canada operates on 110V, 60-cycle electric power, like the US. UK and European appliances on 220/240V and 50 cycles may not function properly. Plugs are either two-pin (flat) or three-pin (two flat, one round). UK and European visitors will need an adaptor.

CONSULATES IN VANCOUVER

Australia: Suite 1225, 888 Dunsmuir Street at Hornby Street ☎ 604/684-1177

France: 1130 West Pender Street at Thurlow Street ☎ 604/681-4345

Germany: Suite 704, World Trade Centre, 999 Canada Place at Hornby Street ☎ 604/684-8377

New Zealand: Suite 1200, 888 Dunsmuir Street at Hornby Street ☎ 604/684-7388

Republic of Ireland: Suite 1000, 10th Floor, 100 West Pender Street at Abbott Street ☎ 604/683-9233

United Kingdom: Suite 800, 1111 Melville Street at Thurlow Street ☎ 604/683-4421

United States: 1075 West Pender Street at Thurlow Street ☎ 604/685-4311

HEALTH AND PERSONAL SAFETY

Canada is generally a safe country, but parts of Vancouver, notably on the fringes of Chinatown and the streets around Main and East Hastings between Gastown and Chinatown, should be avoided, especially after dark. In rural areas, the main health risks are biting insects (black flies, horseflies and mosquitoes).

When camping, be careful with water to avoid the giardia parasite, and consult visitor centers for advice on bear sightings if you are hiking in bear country. Poison ivy, which causes itchy open blisters and lumpy sores, is a consideration when outdoors: ointments are available from pharmacies. Also prevalent is lyme borreliosis ("lyme tick disease"), which causes a large rash and flu-like symptoms and can be very dangerous if left untreated. If in any doubt, consult a doctor.

There is no shortage of pharmacies (chemists) in Canadian cities, and some stay open for 24 hours. Carry a supply of any prescription you have to take as Canadian pharmacies will not accept an out-of-province prescription. You would have to visit a Canadian doctor and get a new prescription that's recognized locally.

Best places to see

1 Butchart Gardens

www.butchartgardens.com

The Butchart Gardens, north of Victoria on Vancouver Island, are some of the most striking and most visited gardens in Canada.

To look at the horticultural displays of the Butchart Gardens today, it's hard to imagine that they started life as a bleak and unprepossessing quarry. Founded in 1904, the gardens owe their existence to Jenny Butchart, wife of R.P. Butchart, a mining magnate who made a fortune by pioneering the use of Portland cement in Canada and the US.

The enterprising Jenny decided to landscape one of her husband's former quarries, little suspecting that her project would expand to include gardens that now attract more than half a million visitors annually and contain more than a million plants and 700 floral and arboreal species.

These species are planted in many specialist areas, such as rose, Italian and Japanese gardens, but also across wide areas as simple decorative features. Some visitors may find the site a little over-commercialized, with its large gift store, restaurant and car park, but it's easy to leave the bustle behind, especially out of peak season. This said, one of the garden's most popular attractions takes place in high summer, when the gardens

stay open late and spectacular fireworks displays are held, usually on Saturdays.

Note that if you are in Victoria for a couple of days without a car, it is possible to reach the gardens either on public transportation, as part of a tour, or by using a regular dedicated shuttle bus from the city's main bus terminal.

✠ 1B ✉ 800 Benvenuto Avenue, Brentwood Bay, 23km (14 miles) north of Victoria
☎ 250/652-4422 or 1-866/652-4422 🕓 Mid-Jun to Aug daily 9am–10pm; first 2 weeks of Sep, Dec daily 9–9; rest of the year daily 9am–sunset
✋ Very expensive (reductions in low season)
🍴 Café and restaurant on site 🚌 75 ❓ Tickets can be purchased online

2 Canada Place

www.canadaplace.ca
www.portvancouver.com

**Canada Place is a major landmark on
Vancouver's waterfront, its combination
of superb views and interpretive walkways
offering a perfect introduction to the city.**

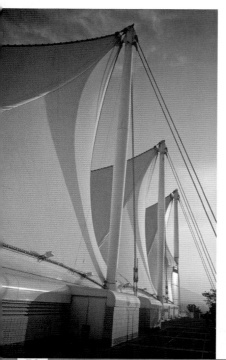

Canada Place was built as
the Canadian Pavilion for
Expo '86, a vast world trade
and exposition fair held in
1986. The event helped mark
Vancouver's centennial and,
for the first time, brought
the city to wider international
prominence. Seen from afar,
the former pavilion is designed
to look like a ship, notably in
the shape of its vast, white
Teflon roof, which resembles
sails – a deliberate homage to
the importance of Vancouver's
port and maritime past.

The Expo event, and
Canada Place in particular,
began an extensive period of
city redevelopment, much of
which continues to this day.
No longer a simple exhibition
space, the complex now
contains a convention center,
the luxury Pan Pacific hotel,

a port interpretive center, and a large-screen IMAX cinema.

For most visitors, however, the building's appeal focuses on the walkways around the perimeter, which offer magnificent views of the port, Stanley Park to the west, and the mountains above North Vancouver, across the Burrard Inlet. These walkways include the "Promenade into History," 44 illustrated infoboards devoted to episodes from the city's past and aspects of the surrounding view. The combination of a central position, the magnificent vistas and the easily absorbed nuggets of history make this the perfect place to visit on your first day in Vancouver.

✚ *Vancouver 3d* ✉ 999 Canada Place Way, Vancouver ☎ Canada Place 604/647-7390. IMAX Theatre 604/682-IMAX; www.imax.com/vancouver ⏰ Walkways: 24 hours. Interpretive Centre Mon–Fri 8–5 💷 Walkways free, IMAX Theatre expensive 🍴 Food outlets in convention center 🚇 Waterfront 🚌 6, 44, 50 ❓ Vancouver's main visitor center (➤ 30) is opposite Canada Place

3 Granville Island

www.granvilleisland.com

One of Vancouver's most tempting attractions combines shops, galleries, cafés, restaurants, people-watching and one of North America's finest markets.

Granville Island is a delightful place, a city regeneration project that succeeded beyond its planners' wildest dreams. For years it was little more than a swamp, tucked away on False Creek, the arm of water that marks the southern limit of Vancouver's downtown peninsula. In 1916 it was drained, and became a flourishing site for a wide range of light industry. Over the years, though, fire and other mishaps laid it low, and by the 1970s it had become a rubbish-strewn wasteland.

The transformation since the late 1970s has cleverly encouraged new light-industrial initiatives, together with a major art school and artisans' workshops, adding a welcome, gritty edge to what might otherwise have become a twee, tourist-oriented venture.

At the island's heart is a covered market, teeming with superlative meat, fruit, fish and vegetable stalls, and all manner of cafés and gourmet and specialist stores. You can also visit the **Granville Island Brewery** and a trio of **museums** devoted to fishing and model ships and railways; ride a converted

streetcar; see a show at the Arts Club; or dine at one of the many informal restaurants.

Come by bus or taxi (it is not a nice walk from downtown), or board one of the ferries that ply False Creek and that also run to Science World (➤ 96) and Vanier Park's museums (➤ 102–103).

🚩 *Vancouver 2c* ✉ Visitor center, 1661 Duranleau Street, Vancouver ☎ 604/666-5784. Public market 604/666-6477 🕐 Market daily 9–7 🍴 Many cafés, restaurants and food stalls 🚌 50 ⛴ Aquabus and False Creek services

Granville Island Brewery
✉ 1441 Cartwright Street ☎ 604/687-2739; www.gib.ca 🕐 3 tours daily: times vary ✋ Moderate

Museums
✉ 1502 Duranleau Street ☎ 604/683-1939; www.modeltrainsmuseum.ca, www.trams.bc.ca, www.modelshipsmuseum.ca 🕐 Tue–Sun 10–5:30 ✋ Combined ticket moderate

4 Grouse Mountain

www.grousemountain.com

Climb aboard North America's largest cable car for a ride up Grouse Mountain, a natural vantage point that offers magnificent views of Vancouver and its hinterland.

One of Vancouver's great charms is the proximity of glorious scenery to the city center, not least Grouse Mountain (1,250m/4,100ft), which is one of the forest-covered peaks you see as you gaze north from the downtown district, across the waters of the Burrard Inlet. Jump aboard the SeaBus ferry (► 90), or board a bus or taxi at Lonsdale Quay at the ferry's terminus, and in a few minutes you are at the base station of the so-called Skyride, the twin, Swiss-built cable cars (they are North America's largest) that carry well over a million visitors a year up Grouse Mountain. It is well worth arriving as early as possible to avoid waiting in line.

At the top of the ride is the Alpine Station, which contains an informal café-bistro and a more formal restaurant, plus a theater where you can watch free film presentations on the mountain and British Columbia in general. Beyond here, you can walk the much-tramped upland meadows, where other attractions include wolf and bear enclosures and regular falconry displays and lumberjack shows. You can also walk short trails (longer hikes are possible), but when all's said and done, the highlights here are the sublime views, which on clear days extend for 113km (70 miles) or more to Vancouver Island and Washington State in the US.

➕ *Vancouver 6f* ✉ 6400 Nancy Greene Way, North Vancouver ☎ 604/980-9311 or 604/980-0661 🕐 Skyride daily every 15 mins 9am–10pm ✋ Expensive 🍴 Altitudes Bistro ($) and Observatory Restaurant ($$) in Alpine Centre. Starbucks ($) at Skyride base station 🚌 SeaBus ferry to Lonsdale Quay, then bus 236 ❓ Reservations at Alpine Centre's Observatory Restaurant include the price of Skyride

5 Icefields Parkway

www.columbiaicefield.com

It's hard to imagine a more scenic drive than the Icefields Parkway, a panoramic road that runs through the majestic heart of the Canadian Rockies.

The Icefields Parkway stretches for 230km (143 miles) from Lake Louise (► 174–175) in Banff National Park almost to the town of Jasper in Jasper National Park (► 166–169). En route it passes an unending succession of peaks,

glaciers, lakes and upland meadows, with innumerable opportunities to stop at viewpoints or to follow short trails (although many much longer hikes are also possible). The drive's high point is the Columbia Icefield, the largest glacial area in the northern hemisphere outside the Arctic Circle. Here you can admire the glaciers from afar or board an "Ice Explorer" vehicle from the roadside Icefield Centre. This is one of only two major stops for fuel and food on the highway, the other being Saskatchewan Crossing, 77km (48 miles) from Lake Louise.

Ideally, you should allow a day for the journey, which will give you time to pause and take the odd walk. Although there is virtually no development en route, the road's points of interest are well signed. Early highlights include Bow Lake and Bow Glacier Falls and their respective trails, close to the Num-Ti-Jah Lodge, where you can stop for coffee (or stay overnight). The best viewpoint is Peyto Lake, reached via a short trail. Parker Ridge is another good, short trail, as is Wilcox Pass. Jasper or Lake Louise visitor centers carry full details of all the trails and other highlights.

➕ 20K ✉ Icefield Centre ☎ 780/852-6288 🕐 May to mid-Jun, Sep to mid-Oct daily 9–5; mid-Jun to Aug daily 9–6. Closed rest of the year ✋ Ice Explorer tours, very expensive 🍴 Num-Ti-Jah Lodge ($), Saskatchewan Crossing, Icefield Centre 🚌 Mid-May to mid-Oct daily Brewster bus service Banff–Jasper

6 Kootenays

www.kaslo.com
www.newdenver.ca
www.nakusphotsprings.com
www.discovernelson.com

The Kootenays is a peaceful enclave of lakes and mountains in southeast British Columbia, full of quaint villages, pretty drives and superlative scenery.

Few regions, even in British Columbia, offer as many scenic rewards as the Kootenays, which consists of two large north–south valleys, the Columbia and the Kootenay. These valleys are largely taken up with Kootenay Lake and the Upper and Lower Arrow Lakes, plus the intervening mountain ranges – the Purcells, Selkirks and Monashees.

Although the lakes and the arrangement of mountain roads preclude an obvious round-trip in the region, you could easily spend a week or more driving the area's many panoramic roads, exploring the rich mining heritage, or taking time in some of the many attractive villages. As ever, in British Columbia, there are also countless hiking and other outdoor activities.

The prettiest village is lakeside Kaslo, followed closely by New Denver and Nakusp (which has natural hot springs), but it is well worth allowing for an overnight stop in Nelson (➤ 144–145), the region's main town. A good base, Nelson is also an attractive town in its own right, full

of old wooden heritage buildings and many galleries and specialist stores. The region's most scenic drives are Nakusp-New Denver-Kaslo, followed by Needles to Coldstream (and onward to the Okanagan, ➤ 149) and the lakeside roads from Creston-Balfour-Kaslo and Needles-Nakusp-Galena Bay.

✚ 11B

🏠 324 Front Street, Kaslo ☎ 250/353-2525

🏠 202 6th Avenue, New Denver ☎ 250/358-2719

🏠 225 Hall Street, Nelson ☎ 250/352-3433

🏠 92 West Street and 2nd Avenue, Nakusp
☎ 250/265-4234

7 Moraine Lake

www.pc.gc.ca

Even in the Canadian Rockies, a region of sublime landscapes, Moraine Lake stands out, a perfect ensemble of water, forest and mountain.

Moraine Lake is just 13km (8 miles) from Lake Louise (➤ 174–175), in Banff National Park. It is smaller and marginally less-visited than its more famous neighbor, but in many ways it is scenically superior. At the right time of the year, when glacial till, or silt, fills the lake, the shimmering water is a sublime turquoise, the perfect complement to the jagged and snow-covered peaks of the Wenkchemna mountains. Almost nothing disturbs this faultless scene, save for the visitors and the well-designed Moraine Lake Lodge on the lake edge, where you can stay or buy coffee and snacks or fuller meals.

At busy times, the approach road is crowded, and the park authorities run a shuttle bus from Lake Louise to reduce the volume of traffic. But even large numbers of visitors cannot detract from the lake's beauty, which you can savor by following the easy trail along its northern shore or by renting a canoe from the lodge. You can also clamber over the massive rock fall that created the lake (not a glacial moraine, despite the name), or follow the

longer (but still easy) one-hour trail to Consolation Lake. More demanding hikes climb to Larch Valley-Sentinel Pass and Eiffel Lake-Wenkchemna Pass: full details are available from the Lake Louise park visitor center.

🕂 21H 🍴 Moraine Lake Lodge ($–$$$) 🚌 Greyhound and Brewster services to Lake Louise Village; shuttle bus from Lake Louise
ℹ️ Lake Louise Village
☎ 403/522-3833

8 Museum of Anthropology

www.moa.ubc.ca

Vancouver's most dazzling museum is devoted to the totems, monumental art, jewelry and other artifacts of western Canada's First Nations peoples.

The original inhabitants of Canada's west coast and northern extremes – notably the Inuit and Haida – were some of the most sophisticated of all First Nations peoples, and produced (and continue to produce) exceptional works of art – anything from the tiniest bone carving and amber beads to vast wooden sculptures and colossal totem poles. Some of the best examples of their work over many centuries have been collected in this

museum, housed in a superb modern building on the University of British Columbia (UBC) campus, designed by the celebrated local architect, Arthur Erickson.

The museum is 20 minutes' drive or bus ride from the city center, but is well worth the trip, which can be extended to include the Nitobe Memorial Garden and UBC Botanical Garden (▶ 94). The building's star turn is the Great Hall, a vast, light-filled gallery built to accommodate the totems and other large-scale works of art. Compare the traditional artifacts here with *The Raven and the*

First Men, a monumental sculpture by the modern Haida artist, Bill Reid (1920–98).

Other highlights include the art- and artifact-filled drawers of the Visible Storage Gallery, designed

to allow as much of the museum's vast collection as possible to be displayed. Other parts of the museum are devoted to art from other aboriginal peoples around the world, while outside you can walk around a fascinating reconstructed First Nations village.

✚ *Vancouver 1b* ✉ 6393 NW Marine Drive, Vancouver ☎ 604/822-3825 or 604/822-5087 🕐 Mid-May to mid-Oct daily 10–5 (also Tue 5–9); mid-Oct to mid-May Wed–Sun 11–5 (also Tue 5–9) 🖐 Moderate. By donation Tue 5–9 🍴 Café on site 🚌 4, 17, 44 to UBC, then 10-min walk

Royal BC Museum

www.royalbcmuseum.bc.ca

This magnificent museum offers a fascinating survey of British Columbia's rich past, natural history and First Nations peoples.

Visitor and magazine surveys often rate Victoria's Royal BC Museum as one of the best in North America, and it's easy to see why. Every aspect of the province is explored, but the displays are a world away from the dusty exhibits of yesteryear. The dazzling, contemporary approach is most obvious in the natural history section, where a series of mind-boggling displays reproduce many of British Columbia's natural habitats. Every detail is covered, right down to the dripping water and cool, dank atmosphere of a marsh on the Fraser delta, or the birdsong and haunting animal cries of the region's temperate rain forests.

Many museums in towns and cities in British Columbia, including the Vancouver Museum (► 102–103), aim to evoke the region's First Nations and pioneer past, but none do it as well as here. Part of an early 20th-century frontier village is re-created, along with exhibits that fully explain vital aspects of the province's past, notably forestry, fishing, farming, silver mining and the gold rush. Vancouver's Museum of Anthropology (► 50–51) may feature the best of the region's First Nations art, but this museum presents the definitive account of the often tragic history of British Columbia's original

inhabitants, both before and after the arrival of European settlers.

✚ *Victoria 3c* ✉ 675 Belleville Street, Victoria ☎ 250/356-7226 ⏰ Daily 9–5, Fri and Sat until 10pm ✋ Expensive 🍴 Café on site

10 Stanley Park

www.vancouver.ca/parks

Few city parks are as wild or beautiful as Vancouver's Stanley Park, a captivating medley of forest, lakes, beaches and pretty formal gardens.

The park crowns the western tip of Vancouver's downtown peninsula, a sublime green counterpoint to the ranks of glass-and-steel skyscrapers close by. One of the city's great glories, it was set aside as early as 1888, when it was saved for posterity in the name of Lord Stanley, Canada's governor general from 1888 to 1893. Thus was preserved North America's largest urban park (it is 20 percent larger than New York's Central Park), an area that in many places looks much as Vancouver must have looked before the arrival of Europeans.

Some is still forest, barely penetrable and dotted with vast, ancient trees; some has been tamed, and turned into lawns and formal gardens; and some has been set aside for attractions such as the Vancouver Aquarium

(➤ 97), **Children's Farmyard** and **Miniature Railway.** There's even a cricket pitch, a lagoon, a lake, and some fine beaches, one of which (Second Beach) has a popular swimming pool.

The best way to see the park is on foot or by bicycle (there are several rental outlets at the corner of Denman and West Georgia streets near the park entrance): there is also a shuttle bus in summer. Whether on foot or bicycle, most people follow all or part of the Seawall, a promenade that runs round the park's waterfront perimeter for around 8km (5 miles). If you want to escape, however, there are plenty of quieter paths in the park's interior.

✚ *Vancouver 5c* ✉ Entrances at West Georgia Street, Robson Street, Stanley Park Drive and elsewhere ☎ Park 604/257-8400 or 604/681-6728 🕐 Always open ⬤ Free 🍴 Sequoia Grill at the Teahouse (➤ 71), Fish House at Stanley Park (➤ 111) 🚌 19 to Stanley Park Loop or 240, 241, 246 and other services along West Georgia Street

Children's Farmyard
☎ 604/257-8531 🕐 Call or see website for hours ⬤ Inexpensive

Miniature Railway
☎ 604/257-8531 🕐 Call or see website for times and special services
⬤ Inexpensive

Best things to do

Great views

From BC Ferries services through the Gulf Islands from Tsawwassen, the main ferry just south of Vancouver, to Swartz Bay (for Victoria) on Vancouver Island.

From the walkways around Canada Place (➤ 38–39).

From the cable car and summit of Grouse Mountain (➤ 42–43).

From the Peyto Lake Viewpoint on the Icefields Parkway (➤ 45).

From the rockpile that closes Moraine Lake in Banff National Park (➤ 48–49).

From Morant's Curve on the Bow Valley Parkway drive between Banff and Lake Louise (➤ 173).

From the three main cable cars in the Rockies' national parks: the Banff Gondola (➤ 158, 159), Lake Louise Gondola (➤ 175) and Jasper Tramway (➤ 166–167).

From a seaplane sightseeing tour or scheduled seaplane service between Vancouver and Victoria's Inner Harbour.

From Vancouver's SeaBus ferry from Waterfront Station to Lonsdale Quay (➤ 90).

From the elevator and viewing platform of the Vancouver Lookout (➤ 101).

Places to see wildlife

The animals may be stuffed, but the **Banff Park Museum** (➤ 158–159) allows you to get a close-up view of many of the creatures that roam the depths of the Banff National Park (➤ 160–163).

Drive the **Bow Valley Parkway** (➤ 172–173), where the marshes and other wetlands, plus a series of viewpoints, offer a good chance of spotting birds, waterfowl, elk and other animals.

Calgary Zoo (➤ 164, 165) is one of the biggest and best zoos in North America, featuring most of the big animals of the Canadian wilderness, such as bears, wolves, cougars, moose and bison, but also smaller creatures such as otters, burrowing owls, whooping cranes and northern leopard frogs.

It's not unusual to see black bears on the **Icefields Parkway** (➤ 44–45) and other roads, such as Hwy 1 in the Banff National Park.

Rivers in and around **Shuswap Lake** (➤ 150) are famous for some of the most impressive salmon runs in British Columbia. You can also see salmon almost face to face in Vancouver's **Capilano Salmon Hatchery** (➤ 78–79).

Visit the superb **Vancouver Aquarium** (➤ 97) in Stanley Park to see the dolphins, killer whales, beavers, sea lions, seals and a whole host of other marine creatures large and small.

Numerous companies in Victoria offer **whale-watching trips** (➤ 131–132) in the waters off Vancouver Island.

Places to take the children

Granville Island (➤ 40–41) is fun for adults and children: the latter should love the Kids' Playground, the miniature railway museum and the chance to ride the mini-ferries that ply False Creek.

The many interactive displays at **Science World** (➤ 96) are an obvious lure for children.

Stanley Park has a host of attractions for youngsters, from the Vancouver Aquarium (➤ 97) and the swimming pool at Second Beach to the Children's Farmyard and Miniature Railway. Don't forget the beaches elsewhere around the city (➤ 64–65).

Vancouver and Victoria have countless festivals (➤ 24–25) year-round, many of which will appeal to children, notably Vancouver's annual **International Children's Festival** and the **Celebration of Light** fireworks festival.

Getting to many of Vancouver's viewpoints (➤ 58–59) should appeal to youngsters as much as the vistas themselves, especially the cable-car and elevator rides to **Grouse Mountain** (➤ 42–43) and the **Vancouver Lookout** (➤ 101).

Museums with child-appeal include the **Museum of Anthropology** (➤ 50–51), where the totems should captivate children, and the **Vancouver Maritime Museum** (➤ 102), with its kids' section. The **Vancouver Art Gallery** (➤ 100) also has special children's events, usually about once a month (dates vary).

Let children enjoy the easy hikes, scrambles over rocks and trees, plus the waterfalls, suspension bridges, salmon hatchery and so forth of North Vancouver's parks, notably **Lynn Canyon Park** (➤ 90–91) and the **Capilano River** (➤ 78–79).

If you can afford it, seaplane tours from **Vancouver** or **Victoria** are thrilling; if not, climb aboard the **SeaBus** ferry to North Vancouver for a fun outing (➤ 90).

Visit www.kidsvancouver.com for more ideas on things to do and places to go with children around the city.

Best beaches

English Bay Beach Snuggle down here in the shelter of one of the large tree trunks to enjoy the view across English Bay (► 83). The beach is a good place to spend a few minutes after walking down Denman Street and exploring the West End (► 105). After the beach, perhaps walk along the waterfront to the east to Sunset Beach Park.

Jericho Beach Quieter than Kitsilano Beach just to the east (see below), this stretch of sand is a good place to unwind or to watch the windsurfers out on the water. Locarno Beach and Spanish Banks to the west are quieter still, the latter rated by locals as the most relaxed of all the city's beaches.

Kitsilano This is one of the biggest beaches in the city (► 89), with lots of sand and backed by pretty parks and gardens, with cafés, plenty of people-watching opportunities, and numerous places to sit, snooze or eat a picnic. There is also an outdoor pool with a gently sloped section for young children.

Stanley Park Third Beach is the quietest of several beaches that fringe Stanley Park, and has lifeguards in high summer. Second Beach to the south is busier, and here, too, people swim in the sea, though most prefer the large swimming pool, which is generally open from mid-May to early September (► 54–55).

Wreck Beach The most notorious of Vancouver's beaches, Wreck Beach was well known in the past for its nude bathing and anything-goes attitude. Things are more sedate these days, but it's still full of colorful characters, jugglers and people offering hair-braiding, reflexology and so forth. But it's also a beautiful beach, with plenty of quiet spots. Steep paths and stairways lead down to the shore from the foot of University Boulevard on the UBC campus. Combine a trip here with a visit to the Museum of Anthropology (► 50–51).

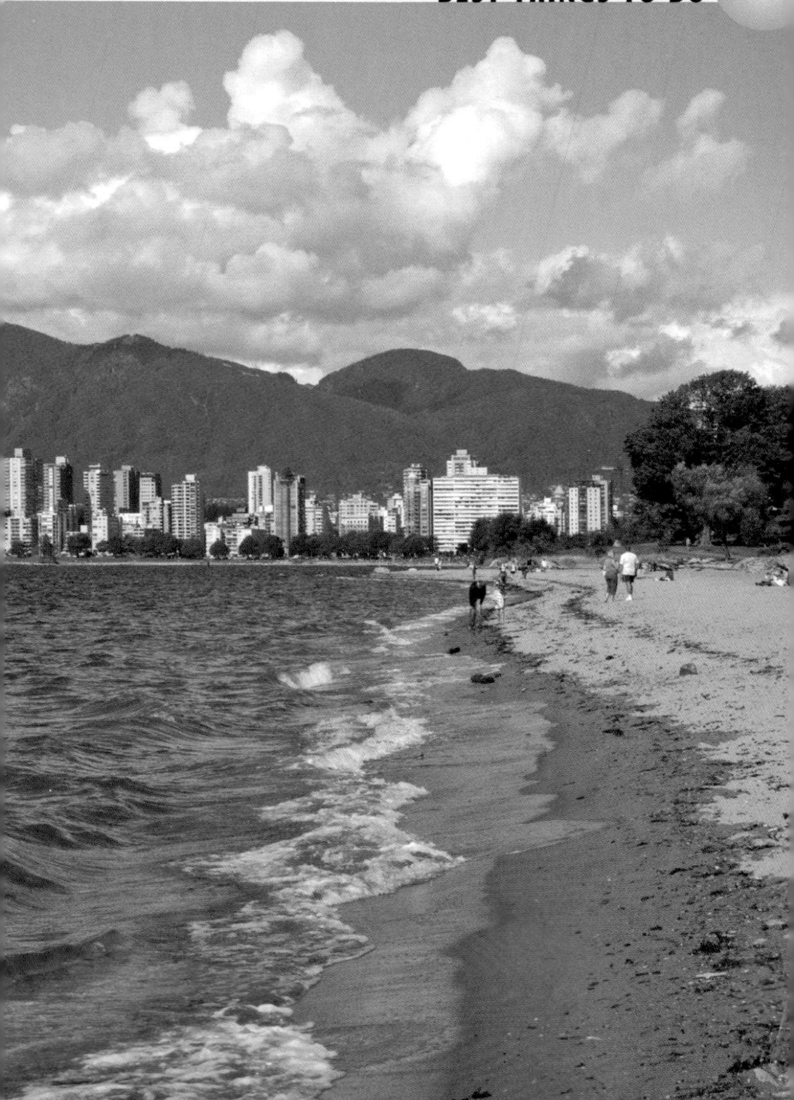

Taste of the wilderness

Take a short hike from Banff – such as the easy stroll to **Bow Falls** or the **Marsh Loop** – to see just how close towns in national parks are to dramatic landscapes (➤ 160).

British Columbia has 25,600km (15,905 miles) of virtually uninhabited coastline: **Lighthouse Park** (➤ 89), on the margins of **West Vancouver,** offers a glimpse of the province's wild seascapes.

The Icefields Parkway (➤ 44–45) may have too many cars to qualify as wilderness, but it provides access to some of Banff National Park's finest scenery: all you need to do is leave your vehicle and walk for a few minutes down one of the many trails off the highway and you'll have a superb taste of the Canadian wilderness.

Visit **Lynn Canyon Park** (► 90–91) in North Vancouver, where just a few minutes' walk from residential streets takes you past waterfalls and deep gorges into the heart of the forest.

A drive along Hwy 1 through **Glacier National Park** (► 140–141), and high over Rogers Pass, brings you face to face with the Rockies' remote world of ice and snow.

Pick a quiet, overcast day, when there will be few fellow visitors, and walk to the **Paint Pots,** a magical spot just a few minutes from the highway in **Kootenay National Park** (► 170–171).

Mount Seymour Provincial Park (► 93) is the wildest of the parks within easy reach of Vancouver's downtown, with numerous trails, long and short, that hint at the immense wilderness beyond the city limits.

Walk down one of the paths that thread through Vancouver's **Stanley Park** (► 54–55). Find a quiet nook amid the towering trees and it's easy to imagine you are in the thick of a forest deep in the heart of British Columbia.

The drive on Hwy 6 from Vernon in the **Okanagan** to Needles in the **Kootenays** passes through wonderfully empty mountain scenery (► 146–147).

The road to the heart of **Wells Gray Provincial Park** (► 151) is one of the loneliest in the province, even more so if you follow the side road to the **Green Mountain Lookout,** where you can gaze over landscapes so wild that some of the peaks have still not been named or climbed.

Hiking and biking

Banff, Jasper and **Yoho** national parks all offer simple and level lakeside strolls, also usually suitable for those in wheelchairs: in Banff, you'll find such walks around **Lake Louise** (➤ 174–175) and **Moraine Lake** (➤ 48–49); in Yoho around **Emerald Lake** (➤ 180); and in Jasper (➤ 166–167) around **Pyramid** and **Patricia lakes.**

Close to Banff town (➤ 160) you can walk to **Bow Falls** or follow the **Marsh Loop**, or bike the surfaced path in **Sundance Canyon.**

On the **Icefields Parkway** (➤ 44–45) there are so many great hikes, the problem is knowing which to choose, but the best short walks are **Mistaya Canyon, Peyto Lake Lookout** and **Parker Ridge**: the best slightly longer hikes are to **Wilcox Pass** and **Bow Lake.**

Jasper National Park (➤ 168–169) has numerous long-distance backpacking trails, but also plenty of strolls (try the easy Old Fort Point Loop from Jasper Town) and day hikes, notably the highly rated trail to Cavell Meadows and the Opal Hills Circuit.

Kootenay National Park (➤ 170–171) is usually admired from the road, but it has plenty of walks, long and short: the best day hikes are Helmet Creek and the strenuous Kindersley Pass and Floe Lake paths. The cream of the easier strolls from the highway are Marble Canyon, Stanley Glacier and the Paint Pots.

Johnston Canyon is the best of several short and mid-length trails (➤ 162) accessed from the Bow Valley Parkway in Banff National Park (➤ 172–173).

Mount Seymour Provincial Park (➤ 93), close to Vancouver, has many good hikes, but is especially known for its mountain-bike trails.

Rent a bike and cycle around the **Seawall,** the walkway and cycleway that circles Vancouver's Stanley Park (➤ 54–55).

Twin Falls is the best day hike in the Yoho Valley in Yoho National Park (➤ 178), but the valley has several other shorter hikes and easy strolls.

Waterton Lakes National Park (➤ 177) has some of the best-maintained trails in the Rockies: the most popular half-day walk is to Bertha Lake from the town of Waterton, followed by the more challenging Crypt Lake Trail. The standout walks from the Akamina parkway road are the Carthew-Alderson and Rowe Lakes trails.

Best West Coast cuisine

⚱⚱⚱ All Seasons Café, Nelson ($$)

This is one of the best restaurants in the Kootenays, housed in a pretty heritage building and with a superb wine cellar. It serves refined West Coast cuisine.

✉ 620 Herridge Lane, Nelson ☎ 250/352-0101

⚱⚱ Baker Creek Bistro, near Lake Louise ($–$$$)

French, Italian and North American influences combine in this log cabin restaurant between Banff and Lake Louise in the Rockies.

✉ Bow Valley Parkway ☎ 403/522-2182; www.bakercreek.com

⚱⚱⚱ Bishop's, Vancouver ($$$)

The chef and owner of this restaurant, John Bishop, virtually invented the fusion of Asian, North American, Italian and other cuisines that go to make up West Coast cooking.

✉ 2183 West 4th Street at Yew Street ☎ 604/738-2025; www.bishopsonline.com

⚱⚱ Earls Restaurant, Vancouver ($–$$)

Earls' winning blend involves mid-range prices, friendly service, first-rate ingredients and excellent food that combines Italian, Asian, French and other influences in best West Coast fashion.

✉ 1185 Robson Street at Bute Street ☎ 604/669-0020; www.earls.ca

⚱⚱⚱ Fresco Restaurant & Lounge, Okanagan ($$$)

One of the Okanagan's finest restaurants, with creative dishes that borrow from a wide range of cuisines.

✉ 1560 Water Street, between Bernard and Lawrence avenues, Kelowna ☎ 250/868-8805; www.frescorestaurant.net

⚱⚱⚱ Raincity Grill, Vancouver ($$)

This romantic restaurant overlooks English Bay and offers excellent and eclectic food made from locally sourced (and often organic) ingredients.

✉ 1193 Denman Street at Davie Street
☎ 604/685-7337; www.raincitygrill.com

▽▽▽ River Café, Calgary ($$)

This restaurant has a delightful setting near the river, across the bridge from the Eau Claire Market. The contemporary Italian-based cooking is ambitious and the dining room is modern and informal.

✉ Prince's Island Park ☎ 403/261-7670;
www.river-café.com

▽▽▽ Sequoia Grill at the Teahouse, Vancouver ($–$$)

A bistro at panoramic Ferguson Point in Stanley Park, with seasonal menus and wonderful views.

✉ Ferguson Point, Stanley Park
☎ 604/669-3281; www.vancouverdine.com

Things to do for free

Browse without buying Sights, sounds and colors are reasons enough to visit Granville Island's public market (➤ 40), Lonsdale Quay market (➤ 90) and the Chinatown Night Market (➤ 81, 114). Gastown's galleries of Inuit and other art are also interesting to browse, even if you can't afford the prices (➤ 84–85, 113).

Canada Place Not only are the views free, but also the potted history lessons on the infoboards on the promenade, as well as the Port Authority Interpretive Centre inside the complex (➤ 38–39).

Cross the bridge It's an expensive business crossing the famous Capilano Suspension Bridge (➤ 79), but there's a similar, if slightly smaller bridge in Lynn Canyon Park (➤ 90–91) that you can walk across for free.

Free art The vast atrium of the bank building on the corner of Hornby Street and West Georgia Street is partly given over to the Pendulum Gallery (885 West Georgia Street, tel: 604/250-9682; www.pendulumgallery.bc.ca, open office hours), where changing exhibitions of mostly modern art complement the colossal permanent pendulum that gives the gallery its name.

Laze by the beach It costs nothing to stretch out or stroll on Vancouver's many beaches: there are three in or near Stanley Park, but two of the most fun are Kitsilano (► 64, 89) and Wreck Beach (► 64).

See the salmon Admittance to the fascinating Capilano Salmon Hatchery (► 78, 79) in North Vancouver is free.

Visit museums and galleries Although few museums are free, several have late-night opening where entrance is free or by donation. In particular, check the Museum of Anthropology (► 50–51) and the Vancouver Art Gallery (► 100), both major attractions, for these evening arrangements.

Walk in the garden... Fresh air and exercise cost nothing in the many parks and gardens of Vancouver and Victoria.

...or hike in the parks While you'll have to pay a park fee in the Rockies' national parks, trails and entry to British Columbia's many provincial parks – notably Wells Gray (► 151) – is free.

Watch the sun go down Find a bench on the boardwalks of Canada Place (► 38–39), or a quiet corner of English Bay (► 64, 83) or Second and Third Beach (► 64) in Stanley Park (► 54–55). Victoria's Inner Harbour (► 124–125) and Beacon Hill Park (► 119) are also good vantage points come sundown.

Exploring

Vancouver is a pleasure to explore, with most of its attractions accessible on foot, and virtually all of them framed by a backdrop that combines the sparkling waters of the Pacific and the soaring, forest-covered slopes of the Coast Mountains. Across the island-dotted Strait of Georgia, on Vancouver Island, is Victoria, the provincial capital of British Columbia, a much smaller and more traditional city than cosmopolitan Vancouver. In British Columbia, the vast and spectacularly beautiful Canadian province that stretches from the sea to the Canadian Rockies, the long distances and large areas of wilderness make exploring more difficult. But the roads are excellent, and in a car – or by Greyhound bus – it's possible to get a taste of the region, even on a short visit. If your time is very limited, however, devote most of your trip to the Canadian Rockies, whose four major national parks are surprisingly easy to explore.

Vancouver

**Vancouver is an
immediately likeable city:
accessible, easy to grasp,
and easy to explore. It has
plenty of sights, as well
as great shopping, nightlife and dining opportunities,
but much of its appeal comes from its setting and
surroundings. Be sure simply to walk in its parks
and gardens, or along its beaches and waterfront
promenades, to appreciate its amazing natural beauty.**

Most of what you want to see is in the downtown core, a
peninsula bordered by the waters of the Burrard Inlet to the north
and False Creek to the south, and capped in the west by the
wonderful expanse of Stanley Park. To the east of downtown
are Gastown, the renovated heart of the 19th-century city, and
Chinatown, which boasts one of North America's largest Chinese
communities. Across the Burrard Inlet, in the shadow of the
mountains, is the North Shore, or North Vancouver, reached by
SeaBus ferry or by road across the Lions Gate Bridge. South of
False Creek, the mostly residential suburbs of South Vancouver
stretch away to the Fraser River and beyond.

   The best place to start a tour is Canada Place, right on the
water and by the main visitor center. From here it is easy to walk
through much of downtown, or head east to Gastown or west to
Stanley Park. Definitely devote at least a day to North Vancouver,
and Grouse Mountain in particular, and to Yaletown and Granville
Island – and the nearby museums of Vanier Park – on the southern
edge of downtown. Farther afield, also be sure to see the
Museum of Anthropology, a bus or taxi ride away on the city's
university campus.

www.tourismvancouver.com

✚ 2C   ℹ️ TouristInfo Centre, 200 Burrard Street ☎ 604/683-2000

CANADA PLACE

Best places to see, ➤ 38–39.

CAPILANO RIVER

The Capilano is one of several short, tumultuous rivers that drain the mountains above North Vancouver, running just 32km (20 miles) before emptying into the Burrard Inlet west of the Lions Gate Bridge. The Capilano River Regional Park protects much of the river's last 10km (6 miles), embracing a medley of canyons, forest and pretty riverside trails. All of it is easily accessible, and is best combined with a visit to the nearby Grouse Mountain (➤ 42–43).

The northernmost attraction, about 1km (0.6 miles) from Grouse Mountain, is the Cleveland Dam, built in 1954, which provides around 40 percent of Vancouver's drinking water. Walk across for lovely views of Capilano Lake below, plus a choice of easy riverside and other trails on the far bank. The best of these is the Giant Fir Trail, but you could equally walk downstream toward the river's second main sight, the **Capilano Salmon Hatchery**. This was built in 1971 to help the river's salmon and replenish stocks damaged by the dam, which destroyed 95 percent of the salmon spawning territory. It

is a fascinating place, with the chance to watch leaping salmon and learn about their remarkable life cycle. Pretty trails run up and downstream from the main hatchery complex.

Most people visiting the Capilano River aim for the 137m (450ft) **Capilano Suspension Bridge** – the world's longest pedestrian suspension bridge. While it offers dizzying views of the Capilano Gorge way below, it's as well to note that the attraction is expensive and busy, receiving almost a million visitors a year. The site also offers numerous tours, places to eat and minor attractions, notably the Treetops adventure, a series of bridges and walkways above the forest floor.

www.gvrd.bc.ca

www.capbridge.com

✚ *Vancouver 5e* 🚌 SeaBus then bus 236 from Lonsdale Quay

Capilano Salmon Hatchery

✉ 4500 Capilano Park Road ☎ 604/666-1790 🕐 Jun–Aug daily 8–8; May, Sep daily 8–7; Apr, Oct daily 9–4:45; Nov–Mar daily 8–4 ✋ Free

Capilano Suspension Bridge

✉ 3735 Capilano Road ☎ 604/985-7474 🕐 Apr daily 9–6:30; May, Jun, Sep daily 8:30–8; Jul–Aug daily 8:30am–9pm; Oct daily 9–6; Nov–Mar daily 9–5 ✋ Expensive 🍽 Café on site

CHINATOWN

With more than 100,000 inhabitants, Vancouver's Chinatown district, to the east of Gastown and downtown, is one of the world's largest, comparable to the similar communities in New York and San Francisco. Most of the area's original inhabitants came to Canada during British Columbia's 1858 gold rush, or to seek work shortly afterward on the transcontinental Canadian Pacific Railway. Many of the immigrants were marginalized and discriminated against, but in Chinatown's clan associations and tight-knit community they found a welcoming refuge.

More than 150 years later, Chinatown is still almost entirely Chinese, full of bakeries, herbal medicine outlets and tiny stores selling exotic fruits and vegetables. There's also a vibrant night market in summer (➤ 114). Most signs are in Chinese, streets buzz with activity and Chinese conversation, and most of the buildings are laden with Chinese architectural details. It's a great area to wander, but make a point of visiting the 1913 Sam Kee Building (corner of Carrall and Pender streets): at just 1.8m (5ft 10in) across, it's claimed to be the world's narrowest building.

Also be sure to visit the **Chinese Cultural Centre,** which offers insights into the area's history, and the quarter's main attraction, the delightful **Dr. Sun Yat-Sen Garden.** It is named for the founder of the Chinese Republic, who made three fundraising visits to Vancouver in 1897, 1910 and 1911. Built with Chinese assistance for Expo '86 (➤ 38), it was the first classical-style Chinese garden in the West, and is a harmonious blend of plantings and space.

Do note that much of Chinatown is rather down-at-heel, and that you should avoid walking the backstreets at night.

www.vancouverchinesegarden.com

www.cccvan.com

➕ *Vancouver 6b* 🚇 Stadium 🚌 10, 16, 20 ❓ Free 45-min guided tours of the garden every half-hour (daily 4–8pm)

Chinese Cultural Centre

✉ 555 Columbia Street ☎ 604/658-8880 or 604/658-8850 🕐 Tue–Sun 11–5 ✋ Inexpensive 🍴 Café on site ❓ Cultural Centre tours and workshops are available (inexpensive)

Dr. Sun Yat-Sen Garden

✉ 578 Carrall Street at Pender Street ☎ 604/662-3207 🕐 Garden mid-Jun to Aug daily 9:30–7; May to mid-Jun, Sep daily 10–6; Oct–Apr daily 10–4:30 ✋ Moderate 🍴 Café on site

CHRIST CHURCH CATHEDRAL

Vancouver's first church service took place – without a church – on Granville Street in 1888, a month before a committee convened to raise funds for the present Christ Church Cathedral, completed in 1895. Offering a striking architectural contrast to the surrounding skyscrapers, the neo-Gothic building is clad in sandstone, but is built on a framework of massive timbers culled from the now-vanished forests of present-day South Vancouver. The lovely interior provides a calm refuge from the bustle of the downtown streets.

www.cathedral.vancouver.bc.ca

Vancouver 3d 690 Burrard Street and West Georgia Street
604/682-3848 Visiting hours Mon–Fri 9:30–4, Sat 9:30–4:30, Sun 1–5; longer hours for services Free Burrard 98

COAL HARBOUR SEAWALK

The building of Canada Place in 1986 was the start of an extensive period of redevelopment of the downtown waterfront, a process that continues to this day. Some of the most striking changes have occurred around Coal Harbour, toward Stanley Park, an area now filled with open public spaces and ranks of attractive residential high-rise buildings. Now that most projects are nearing completion, it has been possible to create the Coal Harbour Seawalk, an unbroken waterfront promenade that provides a delightful pedestrian approach to Stanley Park or the West End from close to Canada Place and the downtown core.

Vancouver 2d Coal Harbour Seawalk

CYPRESS PROVINCIAL PARK

Cypress Provincial park is the most westerly of parks in North Vancouver, approached via the Cypress Parkway (which offers fine views), 15km (9.3 miles) north off exit 8 on Hwy 1-99 at Cypress Bowl Road. Although you'll need a car (or taxi) to get here, the majority of visitors come to walk the park's many trails, most of which start from the car park at the top of the Parkway. These include the easy Yew Lake (2km/1.2 miles round-trip; 45 mins) and Black Mountain Loop (2.5km/1.5 miles, 45 mins, 100m/328ft elevation gain). All the trails are well-marked and provide quick and easy access to beautiful forest, lakes and upland meadows. In winter, the park is a popular winter sports destination.

www.cypressmountain.ca

➕ *Vancouver 3f* ✉ Cypress Bowl Road ☎ Park 604/924-2200, winter sports 604/926-5612 🕐 Daily 24 hours ✋ Free

ENGLISH BAY

English Bay is one of the reasons the West End (➤ 105) is one of Vancouver's most popular residential districts. Fringed by beaches and parks, it is perfect for strolling, sunbathing, people-watching or admiring the sunset. Better still, it is easily seen after visiting Stanley Park, or as the culmination of a stroll along the bustling Denman Street with its many cafés, restaurants and appealing shops. It's especially attractive in the early evening, when the bar of the Sylvia Hotel (➤ 109), among others, is a popular rendezvous. Don't miss the bay's 6m-high (20ft) Inukshuk sculpture, an Inuit sign of welcome and the symbol of the 2010 Vancouver Winter Olympics.

➕ *Vancouver 4c* 🚌 5, 6

GASTOWN

Gastown is the original heart of modern Vancouver, and takes its name from "Gassy" Jack Deighton, a talkative and hard-living publican who, in the 1860s, opened a bar close to the present-day site of Maple Tree Square. In those days, the area was little more than a clearing in the forest, and the bar served the loggers and workers at local saw mills, where alcohol was prohibited. In time, a shanty town – Gassy's Town – grew up around the bar, renamed Granville in 1869. In 1886 the little town was renamed Vancouver, only for its mostly wooden buildings to burn to the ground in the same year.

Rebuilding commenced immediately, but this time in stone, producing the largely late-Victorian district you see today. Much of the area has been renovated, Gastown having fallen into disrepair during the 20th century as the focus of the city moved west to the current downtown core. Today it is a fun and charming area

to wander, many of the bland souvenir shops that opened in the immediate aftermath of renovation having now been replaced by more interesting fashion boutiques, design stores and galleries of Inuit and other art.

Water Street is the main thoroughfare, home to a famous little steam-powered clock, The Landing (a small, upscale mall), and Maple Tree Square, where you'll find several small cafés and a statue of Gassy Jack sitting on a whiskey barrel. A little to the east is the **Vancouver Police Centennial Museum,** housed in the city's old Coroner's Court Building. A fun – and slightly bizarre – museum, it offers an often eye-opening insight into crime and policing in the city, as well the original morgue and autopsy room, complete with preserved body parts.

✚ *Vancouver 3d* 🚇 Waterfront 🚌 4, 6, 7, 8

Vancouver Police Centennial Museum

✉ 240 East Cordova Street ☎ 604/665-3346 🕐 Mon–Sat 9–5
💷 Inexpensive

GRANVILLE ISLAND
Best places to see, ➤ 40–41.

GROUSE MOUNTAIN
Best places to see, ➤ 42–43.

GULF ISLANDS
Not everyone will have time to visit the Gulf Islands, the archipelago in the waters of the Strait of Georgia between Vancouver and Vancouver Island. But if you're lucky enough to be spending a couple of weeks in the region, try to find time to see at least one of the islands, possibly Salt Spring or Galiano, the most easily accessible from Vancouver, or quieter Pender and Mayne.

Even if you don't have time to visit, you'll see many of the islands, large and small, if you're traveling between Vancouver and Victoria. Seaplanes (➤ 28) offer wonderful aerial views of the islands, as do the ships of BC Ferries as they ply the route from Tsawwassen (the ferry terminal south of Vancouver) to Swartz Bay on Vancouver Island (the terminal for Victoria).

All the islands share similar characteristics, being fringed with small bays and beaches, and with unspoiled interior countryside of hills, forest, smallholdings and peaceful back roads. The idyllic pastoral setting and easy-going pace of life have attracted many artists and writers, as well as those seeking an alternative to city living. As a result, the villages and countryside are scattered with galleries, farm shops, organic stores and craft and artisans' workshops.

As a visitor, it's easy to slip into the island way of life, enjoying coffee and homemade cakes at a little café, idling on the beach,

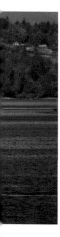

taking an easy hike, browsing the galleries or renting a bike to explore the many quiet country lanes. Fishing, sailing and other water sports are also widely available. Accommodations are mainly B&Bs, or the odd small inn or hotel, and can be found using the official island and other websites (► below). But book early as the islands are very popular in summer.

www.saltspringtourism.com

www.galianoisland.com

www.mayneislandchamber.ca

www.penderislandchamber.com

www.bcferries.com

➕ 2C 🚢 BC Ferries services to all islands from Tsawwassen

❓ Accommodations information www.hellobc.com or www.gulfislandsreservations.com

ℹ️ Saltspring Visitor Centre, 121 Lower Ganges Road ☎ 250/537-5252 or 250/537-4223

H.R. MACMILLAN SPACE CENTRE

This high-tech museum and planetarium delve into all aspects of space and space travel, and provide a failsafe attraction for most children. They're also easily seen in conjunction with the

Vancouver Museum next door (➤ 102–103) and the Vancouver Maritime Museum (➤ 102), a short walk away across Vanier Park. Arrive early, however, as the many innovative, hands-on displays are popular, and the center can become crowded.

Among the attractions are displays that allow you to plan a trip to Mars, grapple with aliens, guide a lunar probe, design a rocket and (in the Virtual Voyages Simulator) gain some idea of what it actually feels like to be aboard a spaceship. The Ground Station Canada theater also presents interesting 20-minute films on space-related themes.

The planetarium offers star shows (usually in the afternoons), but the more dynamic evening laser shows, accompanied by music, are very popular, so arrive promptly or be sure to book tickets. A short way from the center is the Gordon Southam Observatory, which – weather allowing – the public can use for star-gazing at weekends. Entry is free, but check current opening times with the Space Centre.

www.hrmacmillanspacecentre.com

✚ *Vancouver 1c* ✉ 1100 Chestnut Street at Whyte Avenue ☎ 604/738-7827 🕐 Daily 10–5 (closed Mon Sep–Jun) 👙 Expensive. Laser shows, moderate 🍴 Café 🚌 2, 22 🚢 Aquabus and False Creek services to Vanier Park ❓ A combined $30 Explorepass (www.vanierpark.com/explorepass.htm) offers entry to the Space Centre, Vancouver Museum and Vancouver Maritime Museum; buy it from the main visitor center (➤ 30) and participating sights

KITSILANO

Kitsilano (or Kits) is a leafy residential district that stretches west of Vanier Park on the southern shore of English Bay. Now one of the most desirable places to live in Vancouver, it sprang to fame in the heady days of the 1960s, when it was at the heart of the city's alternative hippy culture. Something of the easygoing air of those days survives – one of the reasons for the area's popularity – especially in the many laid-back cafés, restaurants, galleries and specialist stores. For a taste of the district and its inhabitants, spend an hour or two on Kitsilano Beach, a fine stretch of sand, park and waterfront.

✚ *Vancouver 4b* 🚍 2, 7, 22, 32, 44

LIGHTHOUSE PARK

Lighthouse Park is for those who have a little longer to spend in the city, as it is the most westerly of the parks dotted across North and West Vancouver. This said, it is easily reached by bus – it is 10km (6 miles) from the Lions Gate Bridge – and offers a taste of the wild seascapes of Canada's west coast. Vast, smooth granite boulders scatter the beach, backed by low bluffs and stands of Douglas fir and other virgin forest. Some 13km (8 miles) of trails wend through the park, including a 5km (3-mile) round-trip to the 1912 Atkinson Lighthouse that gives the park its name.

✚ *Vancouver 1e* ✉ Beacon Lane and Marine Drive ☎ 604/925-7200
🕐 Dawn–dusk 🖐 Free 🚍 250 from Lonsdale Quay

LONSDALE QUAY

Among other things, Lonsdale Quay is the terminus in North Vancouver for the SeaBus ferries that cross the Burrard Inlet from Waterfront Station on the downtown peninsula. Even if you go no farther than the terminus building, the trip here is worthwhile for the magnificent views of the port and city skyline from the ferry. However, it's well worth budgeting an hour or two for the Lonsdale Quay market, just moments from the SeaBus terminal. While not as alluring as the Granville Island market – few markets are – it is still a great place to browse, with food on the lower of its two levels, and small, specialist stores on the upper. The best thing to do is to choose one of the many cafés or food stands, or to buy provisions from the market for a picnic, and then settle down on the wooden waterfront terraces to enjoy the spectacular panorama of the downtown skyline across the Burrard Inlet. You'll probably also pass through the quay if you are visiting other sights in North Vancouver, for the complex contains the bus terminal for departures to Grouse Mountain and other destinations.

www.lonsdalequay.com

✚ *Vancouver 6d* ✉ Lonsdale Quay Market, 123 Carrie Cates Court
☎ 604/985-6261 ◷ Market Mon–Sat 9:30–6:30 (later opening Fri); dining options remain open later ♿ Free ⛴ SeaBus from Waterfront Station

LYNN CANYON PARK

After Grouse Mountain (➤ 42–43) and parts of the Capilano River (➤ 78–79), Lynn Canyon is the place in North Vancouver to visit if

you want some gentle hikes and an easily accessible glimpse of the city's wild outdoors. Buses from Lonsdale Quay (➤ opposite) will drop you five or ten minutes' walk from the park entrance, depending on the service (or you can take a taxi). Beyond here, on the left, is the Ecology Centre, which offers videos, natural history displays and hiking and other information.

One of the park's main attractions is a suspension bridge over a forest canyon. It is not quite as spectacular as its more famous counterpart on the Capilano River, but it is free and far less busy. It's easily reached on one of the park's several trails, the most popular of which are the 15-minute Thirty-Foot Pool and 40-minute Twin Falls trails. Most of the forest here is so-called "second-growth," meaning that it is forest that has regenerated after the original "first-growth" trees have been felled.

www.dnv.org/ecology

✚ *Vancouver 8d* ✉ 3663 Park Road, off Peters Road ☎ 604/990-3755 ⏰ Park daily 7am–dusk. Ecology Centre Jun–Sep daily 10–5; Oct–May daily 12–5 ✋ Park free. Ecology Centre, donation 🍴 Lonsdale Quay 🚢 SeaBus to Lonsdale Quay then bus 228 or 229 to Peters Road (20 mins) ❓ Free guided walks from Ecology Centre Jul–Aug

MARINE BUILDING

Walk a minute or so up Burrard Street from the modern wonders of Canada Place and you come to an older, but equally beguiling architectural fragment. The 25-floor Marine Building dates from 1930, and is one of North America's finest period skyscrapers, thanks largely to its wonderful art deco doorway and facade. The English poet Sir John Betjeman described it as the "best art deco office building in the world."

Its original owners were shipowners and financiers, and the building was intended as a monument in stone to Vancouver's maritime tradition and the importance to the city of its port and seafarers. Thus the beautifully restored facade is studded with numerous bas-reliefs in brass, stone and terra-cotta, including sea creatures, famous ships from history, trains, aircraft, Zeppelins and other sea- and transportation-linked motifs. The equally striking doorway is often used as a backdrop in many of the films and TV shows shot in the city. The lobby also boasts lovely art deco styling, especially the outstanding wood-and-brass elevator doors and the inlaid zodiac floor.

✚ *Vancouver 3d* ✉ 355 Burrard Street and West Hastings Street
🕙 Mon–Fri 8–6 ✋ Free 🚇 Burrard 🚌 98

MOUNT SEYMOUR PROVINCIAL PARK

You'll need a car or taxi to reach this park, the largest, wildest and most easterly of the protected areas in North Vancouver. You'll also need to devote a day to the park to make the most of its many excellent hiking and mountain-biking trails. If you're going to walk or bike here, be sure to come properly equipped, as the weather can change for the worse at any time of the year.

Mount Seymour Road provides a scenic approach to the park, and runs for 13km (8 miles) to a parking area that marks the start of several key trails. Along the road are viewpoints (Deep Cove Lookout is the most spectacular), picnic areas and several trailheads for short walks. The best of the hikes at the parking area are the Goldie Lake and Flower Lake loops, each about a 45-minute round-trip. The park's most popular hike is the more demanding Mount Seymour Trail (4km/2.5-mile round-trip, 450m/1,476ft elevation gain; allow two hours), which climbs to the summit of Mount Seymour (1,455m/4,774ft) itself.

www.env.gov.bc.ca/bcparks

➕ *Vancouver 8d (off map)* or 3C ✉ 1700 Mount Seymour Road
☎ 604/986-2261 🕐 Daily 24 hours ✋ Free 🚌 SeaBus to Lonsdale Quay, then bus 239 to Phibbs Exchange and 215 to Mount Seymour-Indian River
❓ Park maps can be downloaded from the website

MUSEUM OF ANTHROPOLOGY

Best places to see, ➤ 50–51.

NITOBE MEMORIAL GARDEN AND UBC BOTANICAL GARDEN

These two gardens are a 5-minute and 15-minute walk respectively from the Museum of Anthropology (➤ 50–51) on the campus of the University of British Columbia. The Nitobe Memorial Garden is a small Japanese garden named after Dr. Inanzo Nitobe (1862–1933), an academic and supporter of improved pan-Pacific relations. Now more than 40 years old, and considered one of the most perfect gardens of its type outside Japan, it is a beautiful and peaceful spot, its flowers, trees, rocks and other ornamental features carefully placed according to the principles of yin and yang. Take time to wander the gently curving paths, the Tea Garden (where you can take part in a tea ceremony in summer) and the Stroll Garden, designed to represent the journey through life from youth to old age.

Almost opposite the Nitobe Memorial Garden is the larger UBC Botanical Garden, created in 1916, making it Canada's oldest botanical garden. It has more than 10,000 plants, trees and shrubs, and is divided into eight theme sections: Alpine, Arbour, Asian, British Columbia Native, Contemporary, Food, Perennial Border and Physic. It also has Canada's largest collection of rhododendrons and the outstanding Botanical Garden Shop, full of books, shrubs, plants and gardening implements.

www.nitobe.org

➕ *Vancouver 1b and 2a* ✉ 1895 Lower Mall, near Gate 4, Memorial Road ☎ 604/822-6038 ⏱ Nitobe Memorial Garden: mid-Mar to Oct daily 9–5; Nov to mid-Mar Mon–Fri 10–2:30. UBC Botanical Garden: mid-Mar to mid-Oct daily 10–6; mid-Oct to mid-Mar daily 10–4 💰 Both gardens, inexpensive; both by donation mid-Oct to mid-Mar 🚌 4, 17, 44 then 10-min walk ❓ Joint ticket moderate

QUEEN ELIZABETH PARK

Vancouver's third-largest park had inauspicious origins, beginning life as quarries for the Canadian Pacific Railway (CPR) in the 19th century. After remaining derelict for years, the Quarry Gardens were landscaped in 1930, providing the impetus for the creation of a larger surrounding park, completed in 1939. The area centers on the so-called Little Mountain, which at 153m (502ft) is the highest point in South Vancouver, providing panoramic views over the city toward the mountains of North Vancouver. A winding road leads to the summit, passing through an arboretum that contains most of the trees and shrubs native to British Columbia. Another highlight is the Bloedel Conservatory, an indoor space that replicates the climate and some of the flora and fauna of desert, subtropical and rain forest habitats. The conservatory offers a 360-degree vista, as well as some 500 varieties of plants and 50 species of birds.

➕ *Vancouver 5a* ✉ West 33rd Avenue at Cambie Street ☎ 604/257-8584 ◷ Daily 24 hours 🚇 King Edward Canada Line – opens Nov 2009 🚌 15

SCIENCE WORLD

This is an essential stop for anyone traveling with children, thanks to its innovative interactive and other displays, all of them designed to make science fun and accessible. The vast silver geodesic dome in which it is housed is one of the most distinctive features of the city's skyline, and is one of the key survivors – with Canada Place – of the many striking structures built for Expo '86 (➤ 38). Inside the rambling, open-plan building are five major galleries spread over two levels, plus a large OMNIMAX movie theater on the third level. There's also a special section for children under six, along with regular science shows and demonstrations, usually child-pleasing events with lots of bangs and explosions.

Be warned that the complex is very popular, especially on rainy days and during school terms. It is also a little to the east of the downtown core, so you'll need to take a taxi or SkyTrain to get here, though the latter should be a small adventure in itself for young children.

www.scienceworld.bc.ca

✚ *Vancouver 3c* ✉ 1455 Québec Street at Terminal Avenue ☎ 604/443-7440. Recorded information 604/443-7443 🕐 Mon–Fri 10–5, Sat–Sun 10–6 ✋ Expensive. OMNIMAX, moderate. Combined Science World-Omnimax tickets available 🍴 White Spot restaurant ($) on site Ⓜ Main Street-Science World 🚌 3

STANLEY PARK

Best places to see, ➤ 54–55.

VANCOUVER AQUARIUM

With more than a million visitors a year, the Vancouver Aquarium is the most popular visitor attraction in Canada west of Toronto's CN Tower. At the heart of Stanley Park, it features around 60,000 living exhibits and some 6,000 marine species. Criticism from animal rights campaigners has helped encourage a move toward more scientific research, but the highlights here are still those of aquariums the world over – performing dolphin shows. Also hugely popular are the beluga whales, whose cramped pool has also aroused controversy. Less contentious are some of the underground galleries, where tanks contain all manner of exotic and extraordinary smaller sea creatures. Various areas are also given over to different marine habitats, including wetlands, Arctic Canada and the Amazon rain forest. The aquarium is relatively small, and it can become very crowded, especially around the dolphin pool and in the underground galleries.

www.vanaqua.org

🔺 *Vancouver 5c* ✉ 845 Avison Way, Stanley Park ☎ 604/659-3474 🕐 Daily 9:30–7 (closes 5pm Oct–Apr) 👋 Expensive 🍴 On-site café 🚌 19, then 10-min walk

a walk from the Vancouver Art Gallery to Gastown

This gentle stroll takes in many of downtown's key streets and sights. It can easily be combined with other walks, notably the Coal Harbour Seawalk (➤ 82), which you could follow west from Canada Place to finish in Stanley Park (➤ 54–55) as an alternative to Gastown.

From the Vancouver Art Gallery (➤ 100) walk north on Hornby Street, past the Pendulum Gallery (➤ 73), and turn left at West Georgia Street and right on Burrard Street.

Partway down on the left side of Hornby Street is the Bill Reid Gallery of Northwest Coast Art. On Burrard Street you will pass the historic Hotel Vancouver and then Christ Church Cathedral (➤ 82) on your right. Farther down the street, on the left, is the Marine Building (➤ 92), noted for its art deco facade, and then (on the right) the TouristInfo Centre, the city's main visitor center (➤ 30).

Cross West Cordova Street at the bottom of Burrard Street and walk clockwise around the boardwalks of Canada Place (➤ 38–39).

Canada Place offers wonderful views of the port, Stanley Park and North Vancouver, as well as a series of interesting information boards detailing aspects of the city's history.

With your back to Canada Place, turn left and follow the road as it bears right, then turn left (east) on West Cordova Street.

West Cordova Street passes Waterfront Station (► 104), partly housed in the old Canadian Pacific Railway terminal. Just beyond on the right is the Harbour Centre Tower, home to the Vancouver Lookout (► 101), which provides sweeping views across the city.

Beyond the Harbour Centre Tower, fork left on Water Street.

Water Street runs through the heart of Gastown (► 84–85), the original Victorian-era heart of the city. Be sure to explore its many side streets before arriving at Maple Tree Square, which contains a statue of Gastown's founder, Jack Deighton, and several peaceful cafés.

Distance 2.5km (1.5 miles)
Time Allow 2–3 hours with stops
Start point Vancouver Art Gallery ✚ *Vancouver 3d*
End point Maple Tree Square ✚ *Vancouver 3d*
Lunch Gastown cafés and restaurants

VANCOUVER ART GALLERY

Vancouver's main public art gallery comes as something of a surprise, for, unlike most mainstream city galleries, it largely ignores traditional paintings in favor of often challenging temporary exhibitions and a permanent collection largely devoted to contemporary art – photography in particular. As admission is expensive, it pays to be sure of the current exhibitions ahead of visiting. Little in the traditional exterior suggests the striking modern art inside, the gallery having originally been the city's main courthouse, completed in 1911 and converted by Vancouver-born Arthur Erickson, one of Canada's leading architects, in 1983.

For casual visitors, the gallery's main attractions are likely to be the paintings of Emily Carr (1871–1945), born in Victoria and one of Canada's best-known and best-loved painters. Landscape and First Nations culture heavily influenced her work, which is distinguished by vivid colors and powerful, sometimes almost surreal images.

Plans are under way for a new venue for the gallery in a waterside setting on False Creek's Plaza of Nations.

www.vanartgallery.bc.ca

✠ *Vancouver 3d* ✉ 750 Hornby Street at Robson Street ☎ 604/662-4700, recorded information 604/662-4719 ◉ Mon, Wed, Fri–Sun, public holidays 10–5:30, Tue, Thu 10–9 ✋ Expensive, by donation Tue 5–9 🍴 Gallery Café ($) Ⓖ Granville 🚌 5, 50 to Robson Street or 2, 22, 32, 44 to Burrard Street ❓ Admission free (or by donation) Tue 5–9pm

VANCOUVER LOOKOUT

Vancouver is a city of mountains, ocean and tall buildings, and therefore also a city blessed with an unusually large number of wonderful views and viewpoints. One of the best urban eyries is the Vancouver Lookout, at the top of the Harbour Centre Tower, located between Canada Place and the fringes of Gastown. Neil Armstrong, the first man on the moon, opened the tower in 1977, when – at 167m (548ft) – it was the city's highest building. All-glass elevators, known as the SkyLift, run up the outside of the tower, climbing the building in under a minute and offering a dizzying initial panorama over the city. The views are even better from the viewing platform, which also contains a restaurant (the ride up is free if you have dining reservations here) and lots of information boards and fascinating period photographs that show how the view and its buildings have changed over the decades. The admission ticket is valid all day (keep your receipt), so consider coming back to watch the sun go down and to admire the city at night.

www.vancouverlookout.com

➕ *Vancouver 3d* ✉ 555 West Hastings Street at Seymour Street
☎ 604/689-0421, restaurant 604/669-2220 🕐 May to mid-Oct daily 8:30am–10:30pm; mid-Oct to Apr daily 9–9 💰 Moderate 🍴 Top of Vancouver Revolving Restaurant ($$) on site 🚇 Waterfront 🚌 4, 6, 7, 8, 50
❓ Tickets are valid for return visits all day

VANCOUVER MARITIME MUSEUM

This traditional-style and modest-size museum explores Vancouver's long and vital maritime tradition through photographs, charts, maps, model ships and a wide variety of other marine ephemera. Located in Vanier Park, it is easily visited with the Vancouver Museum (➤ below) and H.R. MacMillan Space Centre (➤ 88).

The best approach is aboard one of the small ferries that run from Granville Island and other points on False Creek. They dock in Vanier Park at Heritage Harbour, so called because it contains a range of restored historic boats. From here it's a short walk to the museum, where the highlight is the *St. Roch*, a Royal Canadian Mounted Police schooner that was the first vessel to navigate the Northwest Passage (the ice-filled route across the roof of North America) in a single season. Youngsters will enjoy the Pirates' Cove and Children's Maritime Discovery Centre, full of interactive displays, telescopes trained on the harbor and fun costumes for dressing up.

www.vancouvermaritimemuseum.com

✚ *Vancouver 1c* ✉ 1905 Ogden Avenue at Chestnut Street ☎ 604/257-8300 🕐 May–Aug daily 10–5; Sep–Apr Tue–Sat 10–5, Sun noon–5
✋ Moderate 🍴 Café in Vancouver Museum 🚍 2, 22 🚢 Aquabus and False Creek services from Granville Island ❓ Combined ticket ($30) with H.R. MacMillan Space Centre (➤ 88) and Vancouver Museum

VANCOUVER MUSEUM

If you're short of time in Vancouver, but are planning to visit Victoria, then you might want to pass on the Vancouver Museum in favor of the latter city's Royal BC Museum (➤ 52–53), which covers much the same ground – the history of Vancouver, Victoria and British Columbia – with more panache. If not, then this

museum does a reasonable job of tracing Vancouver's aboriginal roots and more recent past, combining a chronological approach with numerous themed displays and lots of period artifacts. Particularly good is the section devoted to immigration, including part of a reconstructed ship that reveals the conditions most of the poorest immigrants would have faced crossing the oceans to their new lives.

www.vanmuseum.bc.ca

🕇 *Vancouver 1c* ✉ 1100 Chestnut Street at Whyte Avenue ☎ 604/736-4431 🕐 Jul–Sep Mon–Wed, Fri–Sun 10–5, Thu 5–9pm. Closed Mon Oct–Jun 🍴 Café on site 🚌 2, 22 🛥 Aquabus and False Creek Ferries services to Vanier Park 🖑 Expensive ❓ Combined Explorepass ($30) includes Vancouver Maritime Museum and H.R. MacMillan Space Centre

VANCOUVER PUBLIC LIBRARY

Nowhere is the booming confidence of modern Vancouver, or the degree to which its old downtown core is expanding, better illustrated than in its majestic public library. Opened in 1995 at a cost of $100 million (making it the most expensive public building ever constructed in the city), it is the centerpiece of a residential redevelopment project that is reaching south from downtown toward Yaletown (▶ 106) and False Creek. It resembles a latter-day Roman Colosseum, though architect Moshe Safdi apparently denies this was intentional, and is surrounded by an attractive plaza that buzzes with people and activity. Go inside, if you have time, to admire the interior and the views from the upper floors.

www.vpl.ca

🕇 *Vancouver 3c* ✉ 350 West Georgia Street at Robson and Homer streets ☎ 604/331-3601 🕐 Mon–Thu 10–9, Fri–Sat 10–6, Sun 1–6 🖑 Free

VANDUSEN BOTANICAL GARDEN

Like the nearby Queen Elizabeth Park (➤ 95), the VanDusen Botanical Garden may be too far south of the city center for most casual visitors, but is well worth the journey if you have even the slightest horticultural interest. Many critics rate it as among the ten best botanical gardens in North America. The site contains thousands of plants, trees and shrubs from around the world, including a number of theme areas such as Rose, Lake and Rhododendron gardens. The displays are designed so that there is something to see in all months of the year. The popular Elizabethan Hedge Maze is made up of 1,000 pyramid cedars, each no more than 1.5m (4ft 9in) high so adults can keep track of their children from a grassy knoll as they navigate the labyrinth.

www.vandusengarden.org

✛ *Vancouver 5a* ✉ 5251 Oak Street at West 33rd Avenue and West 37th Avenue ☎ 604/878-9274 ◷ Mar, Oct daily 10–5; Apr daily 10–6; Jun–Aug daily 10–9; Sep daily 10–7; Nov–Feb daily 10–4 ✋ Moderate (inexpensive Oct–Mar) ▯ Café on site ◉ King Edward Canada Line – opens Nov 2009 ▭ 17 to Oak Street

WATERFRONT STATION

Today, Waterfront Station is a major terminus for the SkyTrain light transit and for the SeaBus ferry services to Lonsdale Quay in North Vancouver. The imposing building it occupies, however, was formerly the western terminus of a far grander transportation link, the transcontinental Canadian Pacific Railway (the new bus and rail terminus is now housed in a bland part of the city to the southeast). Behind the imposing neoclassical facade (1915) is a concourse filled with shops, though it still contains original murals depicting various landscapes that passengers would have seen as they crossed Canada on the railway. The *Angel of Victory* (1922) statue in front of the station is dedicated to CPR staff who lost their lives in World War I.

✛ *Vancouver 3d* ✉ 601 West Cordova Street at Granville Street

WEST END

The West End is the name given to the leafy residential district between Stanley Park and the main downtown core. Centered on Robson and Burrard streets, it has always been a desirable area in which to live, but received a new lease of life in the 1950s when the city council promoted new, low-rise buildings in the area to encourage a viable inner-city district. Several older historic fragments survive, notably Barclay Square and **Roedde House,** along with dazzling new developments, notably to the north along the Coal Harbour waterfront (➤ 82). Denman Street is the area's main nonresidential axis, full of cafés and shops, and leads to the beach and pretty waterfront park bordering English Bay (➤ 83).

✚ *Vancouver 2d* 🚌 5 to Robson Street and Denman Street or 6 along Davie Street

Roedde House

www.roeddehouse.org

✉ 1415 Barclay Square ☎ 604/684-7040 🕐 Tue–Sat 1–5, Sun 2–4
✋ Inexpensive 🍴 Cafés on Denman and Davie streets

YALETOWN

Previously a rundown warehouse district, today Yaletown is a completely revitalized area full of trendy loft apartments, great restaurants, boutique hotels and interesting shops and galleries. It takes its name from the laborers who moved here from the town of Yale, 180km (112 miles) east of Vancouver, as work on the transcontinental railway ended in the 1880s. It was a lawless enclave, too rough even for the Mounties to control: it apparently contained more saloons per acre than anywhere else on earth.

Today, the area is easily explored, and centers on a small grid of streets around Homer, Mainland and Hamilton, with Drake to the south and Smithe to the north (the streets to the west and north are relatively uninteresting). Gentrification has not taken away the area's slightly gritty charm, most obvious in the raised walkways once used to facilitate loading from the warehouses beyond.

It's a fun area to wander at random, either by day or night (there are lots of bars for an evening drink or meal) but do drop by **The Roundhouse,** once used to turn locomotives and now home to a cultural center and Engine 374, the steam locomotive that pulled the first passenger train into Vancouver in 1887.

You could walk to Yaletown from downtown via Vancouver Public Library (➤ 103), but another fun approach is to come here on one of the small ferries from Granville Island (➤ 40–41); alternatively, you might stop off en route from Granville Island to Science World to the east (➤ 96).

➕ *Vancouver 2c* 🚌 4, 6, 7, 10, 16, 17 🚊 Yaletown-Roundhouse new Canada Line – opens Nov 2009

The Roundhouse

✉ Roundhouse Mews at Davie Street and Pacific Boulevard ☎ 604/713-1800; www.roundhouse.ca 🕐 Hours vary ♿ Free 🍴 Many local cafés

HOTELS

◊ 2400 Motel ($)

This 65-unit motel is a long way from the city center (near 33rd Avenue East), but is good value and perfect if you are arriving in the city by car (there is free parking) and don't need to be near downtown. Family suites with kitchenettes are available.

✉ 2400 Kingsway ☎ 604/434-2464 or 1-888/833-2400; www.2400motel.com

◊◊◊ Barclay House B&B ($$)

This upscale B&B, part of a historic building, offers six stylish and airy en-suite rooms and excellent three-course breakfasts. The interiors have a contemporary look, with lots of modern art, as well as WiFi and other thoughtful touches. Try to book the delightful Garden Suite.

✉ 1351 Barclay Street at Jervis Street ☎ 604/605-1351 or 1-800/971-1351; www.barclayhouse.com 🚌 5

◊◊◊ Blue Horizon ($$)

The 214 spacious, air-conditioned rooms in this 31-floor hotel were renovated in 2000. They are neat and modern, and have balconies (upper rooms have the best views), though some bathrooms are modestly sized. The hotel has a pleasant café with a terrace on Robson Street, and a good bistro (Inlets), plus the Shenanigan's lounge and nightclub.

✉ 1225 Robson Street at Bute Street ☎ 604/688-1411 or 1-800/633-1333; www.bluehorizonhotel.com 🚇 Burrard 🚌 5

◊◊◊◊ The Fairmont Hotel Vancouver ($$$)

The historic Hotel Vancouver, with its soaring chateau-style exterior and green copper roofs, is a city landmark. This is the first choice among the city's luxury hotels if you wish to stay in traditional comfort but with state-of-the-art facilities.

✉ 900 West Georgia Street at Burrard Street ☎ 604/684-3131 or 1-800/257-7544; www.fairmont.com/hotelvancouver 🚇 Granville 🚌 2, 22, 32 and all other city center services

〰〰 〰〰 The Fairmont Waterfront ($$$)

This is more modern (1991) than its sister hotel, the Hotel Vancouver, but is almost equally comfortable and impressive, and has an excellent position almost opposite Canada Place.

✉ 900 Canada Place Way ☎ 604/691-1991 or 1-800/257-7544; www.fairmont.com/waterfront 🚇 Waterfront or Burrard 🚌 6, 50 and all other city center services

〰〰 〰〰 Four Seasons Vancouver ($$$)

You can always rely on a Four Seasons hotel for superb service and first-rate dining options, and this hotel, housed in a central, 28-floor tower, is no exception. The Garden Terrace is a delightful place for breakfast, even if you are not staying.

✉ 791 West Georgia Street at Howe Street ☎ 604/689-9333 or 1-800/819-5053; www.fourseasons.com/vancouver 🚇 Burrard 🚌 5, 50 and all other city center services

〰〰 Granville Island Hotel ($$)

Although some way from downtown, this contemporary boutique hotel is perfect for Granville Island and the Vanier Park museums, and many of the 85 rooms enjoy lovely city and waterfront views.

✉ 1253 Johnston Street ☎ 604/683-7373 or 1-800/663-1840; www.granvilleislandhotel.com 🚌 50

〰 〰 Howard Johnson Hotel Downtown Vancouver ($$)

The 110 rooms over five floors here are stylish and modern: some have self-catering facilities, making them ideal for families.

✉ 1176 Granville Street at Davie Street ☎ 604/688-8701 or 1-888/654-6336; www.hojovancouver.com 🚇 Burrard 🚌 4, 6, 7, 10, 50

〰〰 〰〰 'O Canada' House ($$)

Ewing Buchan wrote the Canadian national anthem in 1909 in this historic house, dating from 1897. Today, it is a peaceful seven-room, antiques-filled B&B, with a pretty veranda and garden. Children under 12 are not allowed.

✉ 1114 Barclay Street at Thurlow Street ☎ 604/688-0555 or 1-877/688-1114; www.ocanadahouse.com 🚌 5

♦♦ St. Regis ($)

Renovation has transformed this once downbeat hotel, though most rooms remain small (upper rooms are best). The position, close to downtown and Gastown, is excellent, but street noise may be an issue in front rooms.

✉ 602 Dunsmuir Street at Seymour Street ☎ 604/681-1135 or 1-800/770-7929; www.stregishotel.com

♦♦ Sandman Hotel ($$)

The Sandman is part of a reliable chain. Rooms are comfortable, if bland, but there are plenty of added extras, such as pool, fitness center and a lively sports bar and restaurant.

✉ 180 West Georgia Street at Homer Street ☎ 604/681-2211 or 1-800/726-3626; www.sandman.ca 🚇 Granville 🚌 5

♦♦♦ Sutton Place Hotel ($$$)

Top-rated among the city's luxury hotels, and a favorite of visiting movie stars. Regular renovations mean that the rooms are always up-to-the-minute and feature all the latest technology.

✉ 845 Burrard Street at Robson Street ☎ 604/682-5511 or 1-866/378-8866; www.suttonplace.com 🚇 Burrard 🚌 5

♦♦ Sylvia Hotel ($)

The pretty ivy-covered 1912 landmark hotel has long been popular, thanks to its traditional charm and an appealing position on English Bay Beach and near Stanley Park. Book ahead to be sure of securing one of the 112 rooms, which vary greatly in price (the cheapest go quickly). Suites with kitchens are available.

✉ 1154 Gilford Street ☎ 604/681-9321; www.sylviahotel.com 🚌 5

♦♦♦ Wedgewood Hotel ($$$)

The intimate Wedgewood has 83 rooms and is privately owned. Rooms are opulent and spacious (avoid rear-facing rooms), and individually designed with antiques and original works of art. The cosy Bacchus bar is a favorite with patrons and locals alike.

✉ 845 Hornby Street at Robson Street ☎ 604/689-7777 or 1-800/663-0666; www.wedgewoodhotel.com 🚇 Burrard 🚌 5

RESTAURANTS

Bishop's ($$$)
See page 70.

Blue Water Café ($$)
An excellent choice in Yaletown for fish and seafood, with a stylish dining room, open kitchen and "raw bar" for top-quality sushi.
✉ 1095 Hamilton Street at Helmcken Street ☎ 604/688-8078; www.bluewatercafe.net ⏰ Daily 5pm–midnight (bar to 1am) 🚉 Yaletown-Roundhouse 🚌 6, 15

C Restaurant ($$$)
This renowned waterfront restaurant offers first-rate fish and seafood (often with an imaginative Asian twist).
✉ 1600 Howe Street at Beach Avenue ☎ 604/681-1164; www.crestaurant.com ⏰ Daily 5–10 🚉 Yaletown-Roundhouse 🚌 4, 7, 10 ⛴ Ferry from Granville Island

CinCin ($$)
Upscale but informal, CinCin is a Robson Street institution, with fine Italian food and a large, warm and welcoming dining room.
✉ 1154 Robson Street at Thurlow Street ☎ 604/688-7338; www.cincin.net ⏰ Mon–Fri 11:30am–11pm, Sat 9am–10:30pm 🚉 Burrard 🚌 5

Le Crocodile ($$$)
The restaurant's location is unassuming, but the dining room feels like a genuine French bistro.
✉ 100–909 Burrard Street, entrance on Smithe Street ☎ 604/669-4298; www.lecrocodilerestaurant.com ⏰ Mon–Fri 11:30–2, 5:30–10, Sat 5:30–10:30 🚉 Granville 🚌 2, 4, 7, 10, 16, 17, 22, 32, 44

Delilah's ($–$$)
Dine on inexpensive tapas or French-influenced main courses while enjoying the velvet banquettes, hand-painted cherubim and other decorative flourishes.
✉ 1789 Comox Street near Denman Street ☎ 604/687-3424; www.delilahs.ca ⏰ Daily 5–10pm or later 🚌 5, 6

▼▼ ▼▼ Diva at the Met ($$$)

The restaurant of the Metropolitan Hotel offers sophisticated food (fish and seafood in particular) in a sleek and modern dining room.

✉ 645 Howe Street at Dunsmuir Street ☎ 604/602-7788; www.metropolitan.com/diva ⏰ Daily 7–2:30, 5:30–10:30 🚇 Granville 🚌 5, 6, 20, 50 and all other city services

▼▼ Earls Restaurant ($–$$)

See page 70.

▼▼▼ Fish House at Stanley Park ($$)

Superlative fish and seafood characterize this attractive white-clapboard building in a leafy setting on the edge of Stanley Park. You can also come here for afternoon tea.

✉ 8901 Stanley Park Drive at Lagoon Drive ☎ 604/681-7275; www.fishhousestanleypark.com ⏰ Daily 11 or 11:30–10 🚌 6

▼▼▼ Il Giardino ($$–$$$)

This long-established restaurant offers contemporary Italian food in a convivial, villa-like town house with a lovely vine-covered terrace on the edge of Yaletown.

✉ 1382 Hornby Street at Pacific Boulevard ☎ 604/669-2422; www.umberto.com ⏰ Mon–Fri 11:30am–midnight, Sat 5:30–midnight 🚇 Stadium 🚌 15

▼▼▼ Glowbal Grill ($$)

A trendy but unpretentious Yaletown bar, grill and late-night lounge that offers Asian and West Coast fusion cooking.

✉ 1079 Mainland Street at Helmcken Street ☎ 604/602-0835; www.glowbalgrill.com ⏰ Daily 11:30am–1am 🚇 Yaletown-Roundhouse 🚌 6, 15, C23

Imperial Chinese Seafood Restaurant ($$$)

The large, 300-seat Imperial occupies a smart dining room in the historic Marine Building. It serves high-quality Cantonese-influenced fish, seafood and other dishes, including dim sum.

✉ Marine Building, 355 Burrard Street ☎ 604/688-8191; www.imperialrest.com ⏰ Daily 10:30–10:30 🚇 Burrard 🚌 5, 19, 22

✈✈ Pink Pearl Chinese Restaurant ($)

Pink Pearl may be in a downbeat part of town (take a taxi), but it has been in business more than 25 years. A bustling and authentic Chinese restaurant, it has an extensive menu and excellent dim sum.

✉ 1132 East Hastings Street at Glen Drive ☎ 604/253-4316; www.pinkpearl.com 🕐 Mon–Thu, Sun 9am–10pm, Sat 9am–11pm 🚌 3

✈✈✈ Raincity Grill ($$)

See page 70.

Sandbar Seafood Restaurant ($$)

The informal Sandbar offers an escape from the bustle of Granville Island and is especially good for families with children. Spacious and airy, it is spread over several levels. The food is predominantly fish and seafood, but there are lots of alternatives on the menu.

✉ 1535 Johnston Street, Granville Island ☎ 604/669-9030; www.vancouverdine.com/sandbar 🕐 Daily 11:30–10 or later 🚌 50

✈✈✈ Sequoia Grill at the Teahouse ($–$$)

See page 71.

✈✈✈ West ($$$)

Regularly vies with Bishop's (► 70) for the title of Vancouver's best restaurant, and shares the West Coast fusion cooking of its rival, along with seasonal menus and, where possible, locally sourced organic ingredients.

✉ 2881 Granville Street at West 13th Avenue ☎ 604/738-8938; www.westrestaurant.com 🕐 Daily 5:30–11pm 🚌 10

✈✈ White Spot ($)

White Spot is a Vancouver chain that has been in business more than 75 years, and serves well-prepared and excellent-value North American food, notably burgers, pastas, steaks and desserts.

✉ 580 West Georgia Street ☎ 604/662-3066; www.whitespot.ca
✉ 1616 West Georgia Street ☎ 604/681-8034

SHOPPING

BOOKS, CDS, DVDS

Chapters

Excellent central bookstore with more than 100,000 titles in stock.

✉ 788 Robson Street at Howe Street ☎ 604/682-4066; www.chapters.ca

🚇 Granville 🚌 50

HMV

Megastore selling a vast range of games and DVDs.

✉ 788 Burrard Street at Robson Street ☎ 604/669-2289; www.hmv.ca

🚇 Burrard

ART, CRAFTS AND HOMEWARE

Birks

China, glass, jewelry and homeware in a store established in 1879.

✉ 698 West Hastings Street ☎ 604/669-3333; www.birks.com

🚇 Waterfront 🚌 10, 44

Chintz

Among the largest and best of Yaletown's many homeware stores.

✉ 950 Homer Street ☎ 604/689-2022; www.chintz.com

🚇 Yaletown-Roundhouse 🚌 3

Inuit Gallery of Canada

One of several exclusive Gastown galleries selling the best in Inuit and other First Nations art and artifacts. High prices, but interesting even if you only want to browse.

✉ 206 Cambie Street ☎ 604/688-7323; www.inuit.com 🚇 Waterfront

🚌 4, 7, 8, 10

Jade

Sells a wide selection of outstanding jade jewelry and objets d'art in a range of prices.

✉ 4-375 Water Street ☎ 604/687-5233; www.jademine.com

🚇 Waterfront 🚌 4, 7, 8, 10, 20, 50

FASHION, SHOES AND DEPARTMENT STORES
The Bay
Canada's oldest department store and an outlet for the historic Hudson's Bay Company.

✉ 674 Granville Street at West Georgia Street ☎ 604/681-6211; www.hbc.com 🚇 Granville 🚌 5, 6, 15, 20, 50

Club Monaco
Chain selling classic men's and women's clothes.

✉ 1034–1042 Robson Street at Jervis Street ☎ 604/687-8618; www.clubmonaco.com 🚇 Burrard 🚌 5

Gravity Pope
This Kitsilano store is the city's best shoe shop.

✉ 2205 West 4th Avenue at Yew Street ☎ 604/731-7673 🚌 4, 7, 44, 84

Holt Renfrew
Impressive department store; excellent for clothes.

✉ 737 Dunsmuir Street at Granville Street ☎ 604//681-3121; www.holtrenfew.com 🚇 Granville 🚌 50

Sears
US mid-price, mid-range retail giant with a vast store.

✉ 701 Granville Street at Robson Street ☎ 604/685-7112; www.sears.ca 🚇 Granville 🚌 5, 50

FOOD AND MARKETS
Chinatown Night Market
This colorful market opens Friday to Sunday at 6:30pm, mid-May to mid-September.

✉ 100–200 Keefer Street ☎ 604/682-8998; www.vcma.shawbiz.ca 🚌 4, 7, 8

Urban Fare
Trendy Yaletown supermarket specializing in organic goods.

✉ 177 Davie Street at Pacific Boulevard ☎ 604/975-7550; www.urbanfare.com 🚇 Yaletown-Roundhouse 🚌 15, C23

ENTERTAINMENT

BARS AND CLUBS

900 West

The club-like bar of the Fairmont Hotel Vancouver; lots of dark wood and comfortable chairs; especially lively 5–7pm.

✉ 900 West Georgia Street at Hornby Street ☎ 604/684-3131; www.fairmont.com/hotelvancouver 🕐 Mon–Thu, Sun 11:30am–midnight, Fri–Sat 11:30am–1am 🚇 Granville

Alibi Room

Trendy but welcoming Gastown bar-restaurant; the lower floor lounge is for drinks, with good food served in the area upstairs.

✉ 157 Alexander Street at Columbia Street ☎ 604/623-3383; www.alibi.ca 🕐 Tue–Sun 5pm–midnight or later 🚇 Waterfront 🚌 4, 7, 8, 50, N20

Dockside Brewing Company

Stylish and attractive bar that has been serving beer from its own microbrewery for more than 30 years; panoramic summer terrace.

✉ Granville Island Hotel, 1253 Johnston Street ☎ 604/685-7070; www.docksidebrewing.com 🕐 Daily 7am–10:30pm, Fri–Sat to 11:30pm; kitchen closes 10pm daily 🚌 50

Fabric

Gastown club with a great sound system and top DJs.

✉ 66 Water Street at Abbott Street ☎ 604/683-6695; www.fabricvancouver.com 🕐 Thu 9pm–2am, Fri–Sat 9pm–3am 🚇 Waterfront 🚌 4, 7, 8, 50, N20

LIVE MUSIC

Cellar Restaurant and Jazz Club

Red walls, black booths and low tables distinguish this excellent jazz restaurant in Kitsilano.

✉ 3611 West Broadway at Dunbar Street ☎ 604/738-1959; www.cellarjazz.com 🕐 Daily 6pm–midnight 🚌 9

Commodore

Vancouver's best mid-size venue for local and international bands, noted for its art deco ballroom and traditional "sprung" floor.

✉ 868 Granville Street at Smithe Street ☎ 604/739-4550;
www.commodoreballroom.com ⏰ Live music most nights Ⓜ Granville
🚍 5, 6, 8, 15, 20, N15

The Railway Club
Excellent and much-loved small venue; good staff, lively pub
atmosphere (especially upstairs), and an eclectic musical policy.
✉ 579 Dunsmuir Street at Seymour Street ☎ 604/681-1625;
www.therailwayclub.com ⏰ Mon–Thu noon–2am, Fri noon–3am, Sat
2pm–3am, Sun 4pm–midnight Ⓜ Granville 🚍 4, 6, 7, 8, 10, 16, 20, 50,
N6, N8, N9, N10, N15, N20

CLASSICAL MUSIC
Vancouver Chamber Choir
Vancouver's top professional choir was founded in 1971 and
offers a wide range of popular concerts.
☎ 604/738-6822; www.vancouverchamberchoir.com ⏰ Sep–May

Vancouver Symphony Orchestra
World-renowned orchestra.
✉ Orpheum Theatre, 884 Granville Street ☎ 604/665-3050 or 604/876-3434;
www.vancouversymphony.ca, www.city.vancouver.bc.ca/theatres
Ⓜ Granville 🚍 4, 6, 7 and all other city center buses

PERFORMING ARTS
The Arts Club
Three venues, including the Granville Island Stage, offering about
a dozen varying productions annually.
✉ 1585 Johnston Street, Granville Island ☎ Box office 604/687-1644;
www.artsclub.com ⏰ Box office 10am–showtime, Sun noon–5 🚍 50

Queen Elizabeth Theatre
Leading auditorium for mainstream performing arts, city and
touring orchestras, opera and dance companies, theater and more.
✉ 600 Hamilton Street at Dunsmuir Street ☎ 604/665-3050;
www.city.vancouver.bc.ca/theatres Ⓜ Stadium 🚍 5, 6, 8, 20, N19, N24

Victoria

BC's charming provincial capital is the perfect antidote to Vancouver, a small and intimate city, full of quaint streets, gardens, appealing shops and plenty of fascinating sights and attractions. It also has good restaurants and one of North America's finest museums, as well as an attractive waterfront and a delightful old quarter.

Victoria

By seaplane, you could see the city as a day trip from Vancouver, but there's more than enough here to warrant at least an overnight stay. The city was originally a Salish First Nations village, but in 1842 became the site of a fort and trading post for the Hudson's Bay Company. By 1866, this had become a small town and the capital of British Columbia, a role it retained even after the coming of the transcontinental railway transformed the fortunes of Vancouver. Today, the city still has the genteel charm of a well-kept English country town – one of its attractions, especially for US visitors – and is a busy, prosperous but still unspoiled place usually beloved by locals and visitors alike.

✚ 1B 🛈 812 Wharf Street ☎ 250/953-2033

ART GALLERY OF GREATER VICTORIA

If you've seen and liked the paintings of Emily Carr in the Vancouver Art Gallery (► 100), then it's well worth making the short journey to this gallery just east of the city center. One of Canada's best-known artists, Carr was born in Victoria in 1871, and had an adventurous and bohemian life, studying in Paris and traveling extensively, particularly in the wilds of British Columbia, whose landscapes and First Nations peoples greatly influenced her bold and powerful paintings.

As well as a handful of works by Carr, this modest gallery also has an outstanding collection of Japanese art, along with one of the few complete Shinto shrines outside Japan. There are also numerous temporary exhibitions, and the gallery's home, the 1890 Spencer mansion, is one of the city's more attractive period houses. Note that the gallery is easily seen in conjunction with Craigdarroch Castle (► 122), located 200m (220yds) to the east.

www.aggv.bc.ca

✚ *Victoria 4c (off map)* ✉ 1040 Moss Street, off Fort Street ☎ 250/384-4101
🕔 Mon–Sat 10–5 (Thu until 9pm), Sun 1–5. Closed Mon Oct–Apr 🍴 Café
✋ Moderate 🚌 10, 11, 14

BEACON HILL PARK

Victoria is known as the "City of Gardens," and some of the best are found here, in the city's largest park, a few minutes' walk south of the Inner Harbour. In the past, the local Salish peoples knew the area as Meeacan, or "The Belly," because the hill was thought to resemble the large stomach of a man lying on his back.

Today, the park is a mixture of manicured lawns and gardens combined with open spaces and stands of trees, some of them majestic "first-growth" timbers usually found only in regions of Vancouver Island's west coast untouched by foresters. Also here are a cricket pitch, one of the world's tallest totem poles, and the "Mile Zero" marker (the western limit) of the Trans-Canada Highway (Hwy 1). Best of all, though, are the many quiet corners and superb views from the park's southern reaches across the Juan de Fuca Strait to the coast and Olympic Mountains of Washington State in the US.

✚ *Victoria 3a*

BUTCHART GARDENS

Best places to see, ➤ 36–37.

a walk

through the historic heart of old Victoria

Central Victoria is a compact area of streets, shops and squares. To see some of the city's green spaces, this walk can be extended south to take in Beacon Hill Park (▶ 119).

Start at the visitor center at the corner of Government and Humboldt streets. Turn left and follow Wharf Street north four blocks before turning right and up steps to Bastion Square.

Bastion Square is the site of the original Fort Victoria. Visit the Maritime Museum (▶ 126) and perhaps have a healthy drink in Rebar (▶ 135).

Turn left on Langley Street on the right-hand side of the Maritime Museum, then left on Yates Street. Cross Yates Street and take the first little alley on the right to emerge on Johnson Street.

Behind the north side of Johnson Street is Market Square (▶ 136), with its many interesting specialist shops.

Exit Market Square on its north side, on Pandora Avenue, and take Fan Tan Alley, a narrow street left (north) off Pandora Avenue, part of Victoria's once bustling Chinatown district. At the end of the alley turn right on Fisgard Street, then right down the main Government Street. Walk three blocks and then turn right down tiny Trounce Alley.

Trounce Alley was once full of bars and brothels, but is now a pretty, narrow street of interesting shops.

Wend south on the backstreets rather than Government Street, turning right at the end of Trounce Alley on Broad Street, then almost immediately left on View Street. Turn right on Douglas Street, first right on Fort and then first left on Broad. Turn right on Broughton and left down Gordon to bring you to Humboldt Street and the Fairmont Empress Hotel (➤ 133).

Distance 2km (1.25 miles)
Time 2 hours, depending on stops
Start/end point Victoria visitor center ✚ *Victoria 3c*
Lunch Il Terrazzo (➤ 136)

CRAIGDARROCH CASTLE

This sombre Gothic pastiche of a Scottish castle was built by Robert Dunsmuir, a Victorian businessman who grew rich on the back of coal mining and other enterprises. The four-floor castle, built close to the highest point in Victoria, was designed to lure his wife from Scotland, and Dunsmuir spent a fortune securing the best craftsmen and the most expensive marble, granite, sandstone and other materials. Unfortunately, he died in 1889, two years into the project, and a year before it was completed. Today you can walk around the 39 rooms, each meticulously decorated and furnished in Victorian period style. Climb the tower's 87 steps for some far-reaching views.

www.craigdarrochcastle.com

🕂 *Victoria 4c (off map)* ✉ 1050 Joan Crescent, off Fort Street
☎ 250/592-5323 🕓 Mid-Jun to Aug daily 9–7:30; Sep to mid-Jun daily 10–5
👋 Moderate 🚌 11, 14

HELMCKEN HOUSE

Helmcken House is Victoria's oldest-surviving home and the oldest house in British Columbia still on its original site. Built in 1852, it belonged to John Helmcken, doctor of what was then called Fort Victoria and a well-connected and respected pillar of the community – he was married to the daughter of Sir James Douglas, then the colony's governor. Dotted around the house, which still looks much as it must have done over 150 years ago, are numerous period artifacts, including some of Helmcken's fearsome-looking medical equipment. Although British Columbia offers many similar "heritage" houses, you still gain a powerful sense of how life was lived here, helped by audio tapes that use actors and actresses to take on the roles of Helmcken and his family. Just behind the house, which lies alongside the Royal British Columbia Museum, is another period building, St. Anne's Pioneer Schoolhouse, built in 1858.

🏠 *Victoria 3b* ✉ Belleville Street ☎ 250/361-0021 🕐 May–Oct daily 10–5; Nov–Apr Thu–Mon 11–4 🍴 Café ✋ Inexpensive

INNER HARBOUR

Victoria's strategic position near the southern tip of Vancouver Island is one of the reasons for its development as a city, though even its position would not have been enough for a European settlement to develop here had it not been for the area's fine natural harbor. Today, the inner core of this harbor forms the heart of the city, a small but beautiful curve of waterfront fringed by a pretty promenade.

This is a delightful place to walk and sit at any time, but especially early in the evening, as the sun is going down. The chances are the promenade will be dotted with street performers, including the almost obligatory Scottish piper. Seaplanes land in the harbor, ferries from Seattle and Port Angeles (but not Vancouver) dock here, and the city's main visitor attraction is prominently situated near the harbor's northern edge. The Royal BC Museum (► 52–53) is not far away, set back from the water, as are Victoria's two most distinctive landmarks: the Parliament Buildings (► 128–129) and the Fairmont Empress Hotel (► 133), built in 1908.

The Empress is among Canada's most famous hotels, a sister hotel to the Banff Springs, Chateau Lake Louise (► 174) and Hotel Vancouver (► 107). All were built in the wake of the transcontinental Canadian Pacific Railway (CPR), and designed to entice and accommodate visitors traveling by train. Today the Empress has some delightful lounges, bars and restaurants open to nonresidents, notably the Crystal Lounge, with its Tiffany-glass dome. The hotel's six-course afternoon

tea is popular and renowned – despite the very high prices – and should be booked well in advance.

Two blocks back from the harbor, drop into **Emily Carr House,** where the celebrated painter was born in 1871. The building dates from 1864 and has been painstakingly restored and filled with original furniture, including Carr's bed and other period memorabilia.

🚻 *Victoria 2d*

ℹ️ 812 Wharf Street ☎ 250/953-2033 🕐 Mid-Jun to Aug daily 8:30–7:30; Sep to mid-Jun daily 9–5

Emily Carr House

www.emilycarr.com

✉️ 207 Government Street ☎ 250/383-5843 🕐 May–Sep Tue–Sat 11–4

✋ Donation

MARITIME MUSEUM

These days, Victoria's port is far less important than Vancouver's, but in the 19th century, the city and its harbor were a vital point of entry and trade for virtually all of mainland British Columbia. This traditional museum, housed in a delightful heritage building on historic Bastion Square, looks at the city's maritime past using old charts, maps, models and period photographs. It also has a section on the BC Ferries that provide a modern-day lifeline between the province's many islands and up and down its long coast. The building's top floor contains the former vice-admiralty courtroom, which once provided justice for all of British Columbia.

www.mmbc.bc.ca

✚ *Victoria 3d* ✉ 28 Bastion Square ☎ 250/385-4222 ⏱ Mid-Jun to mid-Sep daily 9:30–5; mid-Sep to mid-Jun daily 9:30–4:30 💰 Moderate

OLD TOWN

Victoria's historic heart is compact and easily explored (► 120–121), centering on the grid of streets between Wharf and Douglas, the Inner Harbour to the south and Discovery Street to the north. This site was originally home to the Salish people, who had ten villages in the region, an area Sir George Vancouver

described as "the most lovely country that can be imagined." The first white settlers arrived in 1842, among them James Douglas of the Hudson's Bay Company (HBC), who built Fort Camouson (later Fort Victoria) as a garrison and trading point. Boom followed in the 1850s, when the town became a staging post for prospectors heading for the gold fields on the mainland.

Echoes of these earliest days can be found in Bastion Square, site of the original Fort Victoria, but home today, among other things, to the Maritime Museum (▶ opposite). Two blocks to the north is historic Market Square, the old trading heart of the city, now home to 65 or more specialty stores and cafés ranged around an attractive central courtyard.

The north side of the square, on Pandora Street, was once the city's Chinatown (now centered on a small area a little farther north on Fisgard Street). The oldest such community on North America's west coast, it once had a notorious reputation, and was dotted, among other things, with 23 factories processing 40,000kg (88,000lbs) of opium a year for what was then a legitimate trade.

Be sure to wander up and down Government Street, the city's main shopping thoroughfare, but also the smaller streets to either side, many of which have pretty corners that still evoke a little of what the town must have looked and felt like over a century ago.

✚ *Victoria 3d*

PARLIAMENT BUILDINGS

There's no mistaking Victoria's Parliament Buildings, the imposing edifice at the southern end of the Inner Harbour that serves as home to British Columbia's provincial legislature. The building was completed in 1897, just in time for Queen Victoria's jubilee (at the then astronomical cost of $923,000). The architect was Francis Rattenbury, who was also responsible for the nearby Empress Hotel and Vancouver's courthouse, now the Vancouver Art Gallery (➤ 100). In later life he would retire to England, only to be murdered in 1935 by his wife and her teenage lover, the family chauffeur.

The well-kept lawns and gardens in front of the building feature a statue of Queen Victoria and a giant sequoia tree, the latter a gift from the state of California. A statue of Sir George Vancouver looks down from the top of the dome, while the main door is guarded by statues of Sir James Douglas, one of the city's early leading lights (➤ 127), and Sir Matthew Baillie Begbie, also known as the "Hanging Judge." The latter acquired a fearsome reputation as the man responsible for law and order during the reckless days of the 1850s' gold rushes. You can take short guided tours of the interior when parliament is not in session, but hours vary: consult the visitor center for the latest open times.

🔢 *Victoria 2b* ✉ 501 Belleville Street ☎ 250/387-3046, 250/387-1400 or 1-800/663-7867 🕐 Guided tours: hours vary 🖐 Free

POINT ELLICE HOUSE

Point Ellice House is in less appealing surroundings than Craigdarroch Castle, Victoria's other main period building, but the building itself is a beautifully restored 1861 Victorian-Italianate residence. The interior is among the best preserved of its type in Canada, with a huge collection of Victoriana, largely because the former owners, the O'Reilly family – who lived here from 1867 through to 1974 – barely changed a single detail or item of furnishing in over a century. The best approach is to take one of the small ferries from the Inner Harbour, which drop you at the

dock by the house. When you arrive, take a tour of the interior, walk in the gardens, perhaps try your hand at croquet, and then settle down to afternoon tea on the lawn, weather allowing (booking advisable).

www.pointellicehouse.ca

✚ *Victoria 1f* ✉ 2616 Pleasant Street

☎ 250/380-6506

🎟 Guided tours May–Sep daily 10–4

✋ Inexpensive. Tea and tour from $23

ROYAL BC MUSEUM

Best places to see, ➤ 52–53.

WHALE-WATCHING

Vancouver Island offers some of the best whale-watching opportunities in North America, thanks to its position on the migration route of around 20,000 Pacific gray whales. The creatures pass this way in April and May and from October to December, en route between their breeding, feeding and calving grounds in the waters off Mexico and Alaska. In addition, southern Vancouver Island also boasts minke and humpback whales, plus about 100 resident orca (or "killer") whales. Tofino, on the island's west coast, offers probably the best chance of sightings, but the waters around Victoria are also rich in whales, as well as other marine life such as harbor and Dall's porpoises, harbor or elephant seals and California and Steller sea lions.

The number of companies offering trips has proliferated, and you'll find full details of all the operators at the city's main visitor center (➤ 30). On the whole, it is best to go for companies that

have been established the longest, such as Five Star Charters, Prince of Whales and Seacoast Expeditions. Most offer similar three- or four-hour trips at similar prices (from about $90 per person). The main differences are in the boats offered: Zodiacs are rubber-hulled inflatable craft, and are fast and exhilarating, while covered boats are slower and carry more people, but are more comfortable and have toilet and other facilities. Always take a hat, warm and waterproof clothing and sunscreen, and note that Zodiacs are not suitable for small children, pregnant women and those with back complaints.

www.5starwhales.com

www.princeofwhales.com

www.seacoastexpeditions.com

✉ Five Star Charters, 706 Douglas Street ☎ 250/388-7223 or 1-800/634-9617 ✉ Prince of Whales, 812 Wharf Street ☎ 250/383-4884 or 1-888/383-4884 ✉ Seacoast Expeditions, Coast Victoria Harbourside Hotel, 146 Kingston Street ☎ 250/383-2254 or 1-800/386-1525 🕐 Most companies offer between three and five 3- or 4-hour trips daily Jun–Sep, one or two daily Oct–May ✋ From $90 for a 3-hour trip

HOTELS

☀☀☀ Abigail's Hotel ($$$)

Abigail's is a small, discreet and sophisticated hotel, and feels intimate and homey. It is full of thoughtful touches, such as log fires in winter, Jacuzzis and luxurious duvets. The location, a block east of Blanshard Street, is convenient for the sights.

✉ 960 McClure Street at the corner of Quadra Street ☎ 250/388-5363 or 1-866-505/347; www.abigailshotel.com

☀☀☀☀ The Fairmont Empress Hotel ($$$)

The Empress is one of Canada's most famous historic hotels, and the obvious choice if you wish to stay in the city in high style. It is housed in an ivy-covered landmark building, and while some rooms are rather small, the service and sense of elegance and tradition are what set the hotel apart.

✉ 721 Government Street ☎ 250/384-8111 or 1-800-540-4429; www.fairmont.com/empress

☀ James Bay Inn Hotel & Suites ($)

The painter Emily Carr once lived in this Edwardian building, which has long had a deserved reputation as one of Victoria's best-value accommodations options. Prices are still good, though rates have climbed in recent years. Most of the 45 rooms are relatively simple but the location – two blocks south of the Parliament Buildings – is perfect for the harbor and old town.

✉ 270 Government Street ☎ 250/384-7151 or 1-800-836-2649; www.jamesbayinn.bc.ca

☀☀☀☀ Magnolia Hotel & Spa ($$$)

The 63-room Magnolia is a boutique hotel, and part of the new wave of more contemporary Victoria hotels. The cozy, Edwardian-style lobby sets the period tone, though the hotel is never stuffy. The best rooms have harbor views, but all boast excellent bathrooms, and the spa is first-rate.

✉ 623 Courtenay Street ☎ 250/381-0999 or 1-877/624-6654; www.magnoliahotel.com

▼▼ ▼▼ Marriott Victoria Inner Harbour ($$)

Opened in 2004, this is one of Victoria's newer hotels, a large high-rise building in an excellent central position close to the waterfront. The rooms are modern and comfortable, if a little bland, but there is a good chance of finding space here when the city's smaller central hotels are full.

✉ 728 Humboldt Street ☎ 250/480-3800 or 1-866/306-5451; www.marriottvictoria.com

▼▼ ▼ Swans Hotel ($$)

In its previous incarnation this hotel and brewpub was a grain store, which means that many of the 30 rooms preserve quirky period details from the earlier building. Many are loft-style, or split-level, and all are decorated with contemporary works of art. The one- and two-bedroom suites can sleep up to six, and have kitchenettes, making them good for families.

✉ 506 Pandora Avenue ☎ 250/361-3310 or 1-800/668-7926; www.swanshotel.com

RESTAURANTS

Brasserie l'Ecole ($$)

A modern bistro where the style is good, hearty French food using the best local produce for dishes that won't burn a hole in your pocket. The restaurant was once a Chinese schoolhouse, hence the name.

✉ 1715 Government Street ☎ 250/475-6260; www.lecole.ca
🕐 Tue–Sat 5:30–11pm

▼▼ ▼ Canoe Brewpub Marina Restaurant ($)

A popular brewpub housed in a converted power station – a striking semi-industrial setting. It offers own-brewed beer, a restaurant serving eclectic multiethnic dishes upstairs, plus simpler pub food and light meals from the bar downstairs. The terrace is wonderful, with views toward the harbor and Johnson Street Bridge.

✉ 450 Swift Street ☎ 250/361-1940; www.canoebrewpub.com 🕐 Sun–Fri 11am–midnight, Sat 11am–1am

⚜⚜⚜⚜ The Mark ($$–$$$)

The fine dining room of the Hotel Grand Pacific is one of the places to come for a more formal treat in Victoria. Fish and seafood are especially good (special tasting menus are available), but you can cut costs by eating in the hotel's less formal Pacific restaurant, whose terrace offers an excellent view of the harbor.

✉ 463 Belleville Street ☎ 250/380-4487; www.themark.ca ⏰ Daily 5–9:30

⚜⚜ Milestone's Grill and Bar ($)

Milestone's enjoys a superb position on the Inner Harbour by the visitor center, and offers good-quality burgers, steaks, ribs, chicken, salmon and other straightforward North American food.

✉ 812 Wharf Street ☎ 250/381-2244 or 1-866/468-9658; www.milestonesrestaurants.com ⏰ Mon–Thu 11–10, Fri 11–11, Sat 10am–11pm, Sun 9am–10pm

⚜⚜ Pagliacci's ($–$$)

This bustling Italian restaurant is a Victoria institution, its popularity based on fair prices, good food in generous portions and a lively atmosphere bolstered by occasional live music.

✉ 1011 Broad Street at Fort ☎ 250/386-1662 ⏰ Mon–Thu 11:30–10, Fri–Sat 11:30–11, Sun 10–10

Rebar ($)

Enjoy a range of teas, coffees, healthy snacks and light meals (using mostly organic ingredients), or branch out and sample one of the freshly made juices, smoothies and health drinks.

✉ 50 Bastion Square at Langley Street ☎ 250/361-9223; www.rebarmodernfood.com ⏰ Mon–Wed 8:30am–9pm, Thu–Sat 8:30am–10pm, Sun 8:30–3:30

⚜⚜⚜⚜ Spinnakers ($)

Spinnaker's serves around 40 different beers, including several own-brewed ales (brewery tours available). Occasional live music, harbor views and fine seafood draw a laid-back clientele.

✉ 308 Catherine Street at Esquimalt Road ☎ 250/386-2739; www.spinnakers.com ⏰ Daily 11–11

▽▽▽ Il Terrazzo ($$)

Bare-brick walls and lots of greenery, plus a summer patio, create a relaxed and pleasant setting in which to enjoy first-rate and moderately priced Canadian takes on Italian food.

✉ 555 Johnson Street, Waddington Alley ☎ 250/361-0028; www.ilterrazzo.com ⊕ Mon–Fri 11:30–3, daily 5–10

SHOPPING

Victoria is more a town than a city, and offers far fewer shopping opportunities than Vancouver. However, Market Square, a large renovated historic area between Pandora and Johnson streets, has a multilevel collection of specialist stores and cafés ranged around an internal courtyard.

Tiny Trounce Alley, off Government Street just north of the junction with View Street, also has some interesting small shops. Government Street itself also mixes traditional shops with more modern and chain stores.

ENTERTAINMENT

Victoria, like Vancouver, offers a wide range of festivals and other cultural events year-round. One of the most important is the 10-day JazzFest (tel: 250-388-4423; www.jazzvictoria.ca) in June. Visit www.victoria.ca for a full list of festivals. The city's main performance space for theater and classical music is the McPherson Playhouse (tel: 250-386-6121 or 1-888/717-6121; www.rmts.bc.ca). Details of what's on can be obtained online, from the visitor center (➤ 30) or from the local daily paper, the *Times-Colonist*.

For nightlife, there are plenty of bars, hotel lounges, several good brewpubs and one or two dance clubs. Three of the best are Canoe Brewpub Marina Restaurant (➤ 134); D'Arcy's (1127 Wharf Street, tel: 250/380-1322; www.darcyspub.ca, open daily 11am–1am), an Irish-themed pub on the corner of Bastion Square, in the heart of the old town, with live Irish and other music most nights; and Spinnakers (➤ 135).

British Columbia

British Columbia is Canada at its best, a vast province with some of North America's greatest and most varied scenery, from the Rockies and Columbia Mountains in the east, through immense forests, pastoral farming country and areas of near desert, to the majestic coastal landscapes in the east.

Kamloops

British Columbia covers a colossal area – larger than several US states or European countries combined – and no short visit can do it justice. In an ideal world, you would take several days to travel across the south of the region, between Vancouver and the Rockies, following a meandering path taking in the Kootenays, a pristine enclave of mountains and timeless lakeside villages, and the Okanagan, a mild-weathered region of dulcet lakes, orchards, vineyards and busy resort towns. If you have more time, venture into the depths of Wells Gray Provincial Park.

FRASER CANYON

Traveling east from Vancouver, you have a choice of three routes at the town of Hope, about 150km (93 miles) east of the city. One is the fast Hwy 5 to Kamloops via Merritt; the second is Hwy 3, shadowing the US border (➤ 142–143); and the third is the Trans-Canada Highway (Hwy 1) along the Fraser River.

The last is a spectacular drive (or rail journey), following the arduous route taken by the explorer Simon Fraser (1776–1862), who gave his name to the river, having traveled its entire 1,300km (807-mile) length and passed, as he later wrote, "where no man should venture."

Hope is a charming riverside town, best known latterly as one of the settings for *First Blood*, the first Rambo movie, starring Sylvester Stallone. Consult the visitor center for information on fishing, canoeing and gold panning locally, or pick up details of the many easy trails in the vicinity: the Rotary Trail (3km/2 miles) is one of the most popular hikes, running from 7th Street to the confluence of the Fraser and Coquihalla rivers. Some 6km (4 miles) northeast of the town, the Coquihalla Canyon Provincial Park offers more trails and impressive views of the cliffs flanking the Coquihalla gorge.

One of the most dramatic stretches of the Fraser begins at the town of Yale, 25km (15.5 miles) north of Hope, the Fraser's navigable limit and a former Hudson's Bay Company trading post. During the gold rush of 1858 it became the largest town in North America west of Chicago and north of San Francisco, with a population of more than

20,000. Yale, like towns to the north such as Lytton, is a center for white-water rafting, though most people take a more sedate overview of the river and its canyon (here 180m/590ft deep) from the highway at Hell's Gate, 20km (12.5 miles) north of Yale, and the panoramic **Air-Tram** cable car across the gorge nearby.

✚ 5D

ℹ 919 Water Avenue, Hope ☎ 604/869-2021; www.hopebc.ca

Air-Tram

✉ Hell's Gate, Trans-Canada Hwy, Boston Bar, 28km (17 miles) north of Yale ☎ 604/867-9277; www.hellsgateairtram.com ⏰ Mid-May to early Sep daily 9:30–5:30; early Sep to mid-Oct, mid-Apr to mid-May daily 10–4 ✋ Moderate

GLACIER NATIONAL PARK

If you're coming from the west, Glacier National Park will provide a majestic foretaste of the Rockies beyond, and if you're coming from the Rockies, then Glacier's scenery will strike you as equally spectacular. Strictly speaking, Glacier protects part of the Selkirk and Columbia mountains, which are not part of the Rockies, though on the ground you will notice little difference, either in the quality of the landscapes or the manner in which they can be admired from the road – in this case the Trans-Canada Highway, which bisects the park by way of Rogers Pass (1,321m/4,334ft).

As the park's name suggests, glaciers – 422 of them – are the park's distinguishing feature, and 14 percent of the region is permanently cloaked in ice or snow: scientists have also identified 68 new glaciers forming on previously melted ice sheets, a rare

phenomenon. One of the largest, the still-growing Illecillewaet Glacier, is easily admired from the road.

Mount Dawson, at 3,390m (11,122ft) is the park's highest point, the ice and high terrain creating an often inhospitable environment. After immense hardships, the transcontinental railway was driven over the pass in 1885, but such were the problems with avalanches that a tunnel was bored under the pass in 1916. Until 1962, when the highway was built, the area remained all but inaccessible. The world's largest avalanche-control system is now required to keep the road open.

Stop at the Rogers Pass visitor center for more information on the park and some fascinating insights on how avalanches are managed. There are also more than 20 trails in the park (totaling 140km/87 miles), including some easy strolls from the highway, notably the Loop Trail (1.6km/1 mile), with lots of viewpoints, and the ten-minute Hemlock Grove Boardwalk. Most day hikes start at the Illecillewaet campsite, many of them offering excellent views of the glaciers, the Abbott's Ridge, Great Glacier and Avalanche Crest trails in particular.

✚ 19H

🛈 Rogers Pass Visitor Centre ☎ 250/837-6275 or 250/837-7500; www.pc.gc.ca/glacier 🕓 Mid-Jun to early Sep daily 8–7; Apr to mid-Jun, early Sep–Oct daily 9–5; Dec–Mar daily 7–5. Closed Nov. Hours may vary ✋ Park permit inexpensive ❓ Guided walks from the visitor center Jul–Aug

HIGHWAY 3

Highway 3 ambles across the most
southerly part of British Columbia,
shadowing Canada's border with
the US. It's a strange road of mixed
scenery, glorious in parts, drab in
others, the best stretches coming
in the section between Hope
(► 138) and Keremeos. Travel
this section and you'll be able to
follow a perfect itinerary across the
province, allowing you to combine it
with an exploration of the Okanagan
(► 149) – and thus the Kootenays
(► 46–47) – which is easily reached
from Keremeos.

From Hope the road climbs into the Coast and Cascade ranges
and some glorious mountain scenery, reaching Manning Provincial
Park – one of the few parks in this region – 64km (40 miles) east
of Hope. If you have time, take the 15km (9-mile) scenic drive to
Cascade Lookout and perhaps tackle one of several easy walks
from the highway, notably the 20-minute Sumallo Grove loop,
accessed 10km (6 miles) east of the park's western entrance.

The scenery is less exalted around Princeton, but picks up again
as you approach Hedley, with a lovely picnic stop overlooking
the Similkameen River at Bromley Rock Provincial Park, 21km
(13 miles) east of Princeton. Hedley itself is a former gold-mining
town, now little more than a single street at the heart of grand
countryside. The small but interesting **Hedley Museum** (which
also offers visitor information) has archive photographs and
displays on the region's mining heritage.

At rustic little Keremeos, a quaint and highly recommended
stopover, the landscape changes again, becoming far more
pastoral, thanks to a balmy climate that provides one of the

longest growing seasons in Canada. As a result, this is fruit and vegetable country, the town being cradled by lush orchards, its fertile, narrow plain surrounded by pretty hills and mountains. Roadside stands sell all manner of fruit in season, while the **St. Laszlo Vineyard,** 1km (0.6 miles) east of the town, offers tours and tastings.

www.env.gov.bc.ca/bcparks

www.similkameencountry.org

➕ 6B

Hedley Museum

✉ 712 Daly Street, Hedley ☎ 250/292-8422 🕐 Mid-May to Aug daily 9–5; Sep to mid-May Thu–Mon 9–4 ✋ Donation

St. Laszlo Vineyard

✉ 2605 Hwy 3, Site 95, Comp 8, Keremeos, BC, V0X 1N0 ☎ 250/499-2856 🕐 Daily 9–9

NELSON

British Columbia has some of the world's most beautiful scenery, but its towns, with one or two exceptions, are often functional, modern places. The most notable exception is Nelson (population 10,000), the main town of the Kootenays (► 46–47) region in the southeast of the province. An attractive and easy-going place, it has a hilly lakeside setting and more than 350 pretty wooden "heritage" houses (the town was memorably used as the setting for Steve Martin's film *Roxanne*). Over the years it has attracted numerous artists and writers (more per head of population than anywhere else in Canada), creating a lively arts and cultural scene, and a civilized town with a close-knit sense of community. There is also a respected art college, a school of Chinese medicine and a **museum.**

The result is a place with lots of cafés, galleries, bookshops and vintage clothes stores, making its grid of tree-lined streets a pleasure to browse and explore. In summer, Artwalk links a hundred or so of the town's galleries and studios: you can obtain details from the visitor center, which also has pamphlets on walks and drives around the area's heritage buildings. Another walk, to Pulpit Rock (1 hour), offers a lovely view of the town from the north side of Kootenay Lake. In summer, the town also offers a farmers' market (Saturdays in Cottonwood Falls Park) and a restored streetcar that runs along the lakeshore.

Out of town, the lakes, mountains and scenic drives of the Kootenays are virtually on the doorstep. Don't miss Kokanee

Glacier Provincial Park, 35km (21.5 miles) northeast of the town, with many hiking trails, long and short: some of the best (notably to Kokanee Lake) start from the Gibson Lake parking area, one of the park's entry points.

➕ 11B

ℹ️ 225 Hall Street ☎ 250/352-3433 or 1-877/663-5706 🕐 Jun–Aug daily 8:30–6; Sep–May Mon–Fri 8:30–5

Nelson Museum

✉️ 502 Vernon Street ☎ 250/352-9813 🕐 Mon–Sat 9–5

a drive through the heart of British Columbia

This is one of countless scenic drives in Western Canada, and a route that links – assuming you are on a tour across the region – three of the key areas of central BC: the Okanagan, Kootenays and Cascade and Columbia mountains.

Start at Vernon, the northernmost of the main towns in the Okanagan (➤ 149). Take Hwy 6 east toward Lumby, Cherryville and Needles.

Out of Vernon the highway glides through sublime pastoral landscapes of orchards, meadows and low, tree-covered hills. Beyond the settlements of Lumby and Cherryville it climbs into the Monashee Mountains (www.monasheetourism.com), passing through empty countryside before cresting the Monashee Pass (1,198m/3,930ft) and dropping into the Coldstream Valley for the ferry crossing at Needles on Lower Arrow Lake.

Take the five-minute ferry crossing to tiny Fauquier, which has the only motel and restaurant in the area (Arrow Lake Motel, tel: 250/269-7622) and continue north on Hwy 6 for 57km (35 miles) to Nakusp. If you are short of time, continue north via the ferry crossing at Galena Bay to Revelstoke. If not, drive east to Kaslo on Hwy 6 via New Denver.

Lakeside Nakusp in the Kootenays (➤ 46–47) makes a delightful stop for food or an overnight stay, as does backwoods New Denver, 47km (30 miles) to the east, a former silver-mining town with another fine lakeside setting. The road between the two is a wonderful drive through majestic mountain scenery, only bettered by the drive from New Denver to Kaslo (➤ 46), one of the most scenic stretches of road in the province.

It is 150km (93 miles) from Kaslo to Revelstoke via Gerrard and Galena Bay, a wild and dramatic route along mostly gravel road, so be sure to have a full tank of gas. Revelstoke has plenty of accommodations and leaves you well placed to head east toward the Rockies on Hwy 1 via Glacier National Park (➤ 140–141).

Distance 300km/186 miles (460km/285 miles via Kaslo)
Time 1–3 days
Start point Vernon ✚ 8D
End point Revelstoke ✚ 10E
Overnight stop Nakusp (➤ 154)

KAMLOOPS

Kamloop's position, 355km (220 miles) from Vancouver, on several major highways and close to the center of southern British Columbia, means that it is a town you are likely to pass through on any number of itineraries across the province. Its outskirts sprawl in all directions across bare, sun-baked brown hills and arid river plains, with plenty of inexpensive accommodations options if you wish to break your journey. The old town center is more appealing, home to a pair of small historical museums, galleries of contemporary art and the **Kamloops Heritage Railway,** which offers visitors a 70-minute steam-train ride in the summer months.

🞧 7E

🛈 1290 West Trans-Canada Hwy ☎ 250/374-3377; www.tourismkamloops.com

Kamloops Heritage Railway

✉ 510 Lorne Street ☎ 250/374-2141; www.kamrail.com 🕓 Departures Jul–Aug Fri–Mon ✋ Moderate

KOOTENAYS

Best places to see, ➤ 46–47.

OKANAGAN

The Okanagan comes as a surprise after the forests and snow-dusted mountains of much of British Columbia. A region of lakes and low hills, its marked microclimate – with hot summers and mild winters – allows for the growing of grapes, peaches and other warm-weather fruit. As a result, this is a pretty, pastoral corner, at least in its rural hinterland, for the region's lakeside towns, and Kelowna in particular, are big, booming places, popular as summer resorts and with a bustle uncharacteristic of British Columbia. Many US and Canadian visitors come here to idle by the lakes in July and August, but the best times to visit are in spring, when the fruit trees are in blossom, or in autumn, when the leaves are turning and the grape harvest begins. The region's other towns, Vernon and Penticton, resemble Kelowna, with sprawling, unattractive suburbs but pretty, well-kept centers. Vernon is close to the region's key historic sight, the **O'Keefe Ranch,** a collection of historic buildings that vividly evoke 19th-century pioneer life. You could easily see much of the region passing through, or in a day or two's driving, preferably on the quieter roads on the western side of Lake Okanagan.

✚ 8C

🛈 544 Harvey Avenue, Kelowna

☎ 250/861-1515; www.tourismkelowna.com

🛈 533 Railway Street, Penticton

☎ 250/493-4055; www.tourismpenticton.ca

🛈 701 Hwy 97, Vernon ☎ 250/542-1415; www.vernontourism.com

O'Keefe Ranch

✉ 12km (7.5 miles) north of Vernon, off Hwy 97 ☎ 250/542-7868; www.okeeferanch.ca 🕒 Jul–Aug daily 9–8; May, Jun, Sep to mid-Oct daily 9–5

✋ Moderate

SHUSWAP LAKE

Shuswap Lake comprises more than 1,000km (620 miles) of navigable waterways, part of an intermittently pretty corner of British Columbia between Kamloops to the west and the Monashee Mountains to the east. Most people drive along much of its length as they follow the Trans-Canada Highway. Its hinterland is filled with small provincial parks, crammed with fishing, hiking and other outdoor possibilities, but it is best known for the little town of Salmon Arm, 108km (67 miles) east of Kamloops. As its name suggests, this is a place associated with fish, for Shuswap Lake provides an important link in the Fraser and Thompson river systems, and is the most important salmon habitat in North America. In spawning season, in October, millions of fish pass through local rivers, attracting vast numbers of visitors who come to watch the spectacle.

✚ 17H

ℹ 200 Trans-Canada Highway, Salmon Arm ☎ 250/832-2230; www.csrd.bc.ca

WELLS GRAY PROVINCIAL PARK

Wells Gray is one of British Columbia's most enticing parks, on a scenic par with the better-known parks of the Canadian Rockies to the east. Its southern reaches are easily accessed from scenic Hwy 5 from Kamloops to Tête Jaune Cache (338km/210 miles) where you can pick up Hwy 16 east to Jasper, making the park a good stop off as part of a longer itinerary.

Drive north from Kamloops and you can access Sun Peaks Resort after 53km (33 miles), BC's second-largest winter sports destination after Whistler (it also offers plenty of hiking and other activities in the summer). Clearwater, 125km (77 miles) north of Kamloops, provides a good base for a day trip exploring the park, which is accessed from Hwy 5 via a 78km (48.5-mile) access road.

About 10km (6 miles) north of Clearwater on this road is Spahats Falls, one of several impressive waterfalls in the park. Just beyond the park entrance is a turnoff to Green Mountain Lookout, which provides a great viewpoint over a vast expanse of wilderness. Dawson Falls is the next major signposted sight, five minutes' walk from the road, followed by the trailhead for the Murtle River Trail (14km/8.7 miles), which offers more waterfalls. Close by is the turnoff for Helmcken Falls, the park's highlight, a cascade that, at 137m (450ft) high, is more than twice the height of Niagara Falls. Also see Ray Farm (1912), the picturesque former home of John Bunyon Ray, a former homesteader.

The park road ends at pretty Clearwater Lake, where you can rent canoes, camp or walk several easy short trails. Rafting trips on the Clearwater River can also be booked from several operators in Clearwater.

✚ 16L

🛈 Sun Peaks Resort ☎ 1-800/807-3257; www.sunpeaksresort.com

🛈 Hwy 5, Clearwater ☎ 250/674-2646; www.clearwaterbcchamber.com

WHISTLER

Whistler, the main focus of the 2010 Winter Olympic Games, is one of North America's premier recreational resorts. Set at the heart of the spectacular Coast Mountains, it lies within easy reach of Vancouver, just 125km (77 miles) to the south, connected by a major highway (Hwy 99) and with regular bus services from the city. Traditionally it has been seen as a winter sports resort, its activities centered on two mountains, Whistler and Blackcomb, with some of North America's longest, highest and most varied ski runs (suitable for all abilities), as well as boarding, sledging, snow-shoeing, dog-sled tours, snowmobiling and other activities.

More recently, however, it has emerged as a summer resort, with mountain-biking, in particular, a major activity. However, there are plenty of other activities, for all ages and abilities, and casual visitors can easily rent bicycles (and other outdoor equipment) in Whistler Village, the resort's purpose-built modern center. Hiking is excellent, with cable cars allowing walkers easy access to high-level trails. There are also four major golf courses locally (visit www.golfbc.com for more information), plus fishing, jet-boating and rafting, and a host of other activities. Visitor centers carry all the information you need to choose, book or pursue an activity.

www.tourismwhistler.com

www.whistlerchamber.com

www.whistlerblackcomb.com

✚ 3E

🛈 4010 Whistler Way, Whistler Village Square, tel: 604/932-3928 or 1-888/869-2777. Chamber of Commerce, 4230 Gateway Drive, Whistler Village

HOTELS

FRASER CANYON
⚜⚜ Skagit Motor Inn ($)
The Skagit's ground-level rooms (with parking outside) are bright and light, with modern fittings and furniture. The low-rise, single-story motel also occupies a pretty and peaceful spot.

✉ 655 3rd Avenue, Hope ☎ 604/869-5220 or 1-888/869-5228; www.skagit-motor-inn.com

GLACIER NATIONAL PARK
⚜⚜⚜ Kapristo Lodge ($$)
Glacier National Park has just two small hotel options (Glacier Park Lodge and Heather Mountain Lodge), both of which tend to be full in high season. Most visitors choose to stay outside the park in Golden, 54km (34 miles) from Field, which has far greater choice: the best option is the Kapristo Lodge, a lovely modern wooden complex 10 minutes south of Golden in extensive wooded grounds overlooking the Columbia River.

✉ 1297 Campbell Road, Golden ☎ 250/344-6048 or 1-866/767-9630; www.kapristolodge.com

HIGHWAY 3
⚜⚜⚜ Best Western Princeton Inn ($)
This modern hotel is just off the main highway on the eastern fringe of Princeton, about 10 minutes' walk to the center.

✉ 169 Hwy 3, Princeton ☎ 250/295-3537 or 1-800/780-7234; www.bestwesternbc.com/princeton-hotels

KASLO
Kaslo Motel ($)
Kaslo is one of British Columbia's most delightful small towns, but has few places to stay (there are more options up and down the lake north and south of the town). However, this well-run and long-established motel is central, and its quaint, brightly painted cabins make an ideal base for the town and the surroundings.

✉ 330 D Avenue, Kaslo ☎ 250/353-2431, 1-877/353 2431 or 1-877/353 2431; www.kaslomotel.ca

NAKUSP
♨♨ The Selkirk Inn ($)
This simple but amenable motel-style lodging, with spacious rooms, is the pick of the handful of places to stay in Nakusp.
✉ 210 6th Avenue West, Nakusp ☎ 250/265-3666 or 1-800/661-8007; www.selkirkinn-nakusp.com

NELSON
♨♨♨ Best Western Baker Street Inn ($$)
You will want to explore Nelson on foot from your hotel, so plump for one of the 70 rooms here, which are more modern and stylish than most of the places to stay in downtown Nelson.
✉ 153 Baker Street ☎ 250/352-3525 or 1-888/255-3525; www.bwbakerstreetinn.com

OKANAGAN
♨♨♨ Lake Okanagan Resort ($–$$)
For a treat, base yourself at this beautiful self-contained resort, with golf course, tennis courts, horse-back riding, private beach, pools and 125 rooms, most of which are on the lakeside.
✉ 2751 Westside Road, Kelowna ☎ 250/769-3511 or 1-800/663-3273; www.lakeokanagan.com

WELLS GRAY PROVINCIAL PARK
♨♨ Dutch Lake Motel and Campground ($)
In a pretty and peaceful position on Dutch Lake, this motel is also convenient for the access road into the park. Choose from a variety of pretty waterfront cabins.
✉ 333 Roy Road, Clearwater ☎ 250/674-3325 or 1-877/674-3325; www.dutchlakemotel.com

WHISTLER
Executive Inn ($–$$)
This European chalet-style hotel is one of the best-value places to stay at the heart of Whistler Village.
✉ 4250 Village Stroll, Whistler ☎ 604/932-3200 or 1-800/663-6416; www.executiveinnwhistler.com

RESTAURANTS

GOLDEN
▽▽▽ Kicking Horse Grill ($$)
The contemporary Canadian food here is superb, but so, too, is the delightful setting – in a cozy old log cabin.

✉ 1105 9th Street South ☎ 250/344 2330; www.thekickinghorsegrill.ca
🕐 Daily 5–10pm

HIGHWAY 3
▽▽ Home Restaurant ($)
Home started as a simple roadside diner in 1953, and it still adheres to a formula of old-style home cooking (all the recipes claim to be more than 50 years old).

✉ 665 Old Hope-Princeton Way, Hope ☎ 604/869 5558;
www.homerestaurants.ca

KASLO
Rosewood Café ($$)
A restored pink-colored heritage building, crammed with antiques, is the setting for this popular and informal café-restaurant serving quality soups, sandwiches, pastas and other light meals.

✉ 213 5th Street, Kaslo ☎ 250/353 7673 🕐 Mon–Sat 11–9, Sun 9:30–9

NELSON
▽▽▽ All Seasons Café ($$)
See page 70.

▽ Thor's Pizza & Subs ($)
Nelson has numerous inexpensive dining options, but if you want pizza, then Thor's should be your first port of call.

✉ 303 Victoria Street ☎ 250/352 1212; www.ilovenelson.com/thors
🕐 Mon–Thu 11–10, Fri–Sat 11am–midnight, Sun 4–9pm

OKANAGAN
▽▽▽ Bouchons Bistro ($$$)
Bouchons offers first-rate French fine dining at bistro prices, with excellent versions of classic Gallic dishes such as duck confit and

medallions of rabbit, and prime Albertan steak, plus an excellent wine list.

✉ 105-1180 Sunset Drive, Kelowna ☎ 250/763-6595; www.bouchonsbistro.com 🕒 Daily 5:30–10pm. Closed mid-Feb to mid-Mar

▼▼▼▼ Fresco Restaurant & Lounge ($$$)
See page 70.

SHUSWAP LAKE
▼▼ Primavera Ristorante Italiano ($)
There are few frills at this family-friendly restaurant, but the Italian food is some of the best in the region.

✉ 260 Ross Street NE, Salmon Arm ☎ 250/833-0065
🕒 Mon 5:30–10:30pm, Tue–Fri 12:30–2:30, 5:30–10:30, Sat 5:30–10:30. Closed Sun

WELLS GRAY PROVINCIAL PARK
Helmcken Falls Lodge ($)
This isolated and historic wooden lodge is virtually the only place to eat inside the park itself, and serves hearty breakfasts and lunches and dinners of robust Canadian and European dishes. There are also rooms if you wish to stay the night.

✉ 35km (21 miles) from Hwy 5–Clearwater off the park entrance road
☎ 250/674-3657; www.helmckenfalls.com 🕒 Daily 7am–10pm

WHISTLER
▼▼▼ Araxi ($$$)
Long-established favorite, with accomplished and often innovative Italian and West Coast cooking, plus a seafood bar.

✉ 4222 Village Square ☎ 604/932-4540; www.araxi.com 🕒 Daily 5–11pm

Ingrid's Village Café ($)
Join locals and resort workers in Whistler's most popular café for coffee, wraps, sandwiches and daily specials at good prices.

✉ 4305 Skiers' Approach-Village Square ☎ 604/932-7000; www.ingridswhistler.com 🕒 Daily from 7:30am

The Rockies

The Canadian Rockies are one of the world's great landscapes, a sublime medley of mountains, forests, lakes, rivers and glaciers that combines vast swathes of wilderness with almost limitless opportunities for hiking, mountain biking, fishing, winter sports and other outdoor activities.

Calgary

The range stretches from the border with the United States almost to the Yukon in Canada's far north, straddling the provinces of Alberta and British Columbia, but the area most people visit is in the south, in the Rockies' four adjoining national parks: Banff and Jasper, the two largest, and Kootenay and Yoho, both much smaller, but with scenery that is every bit as impressive. Fantastic scenic roads run through all four parks, notably the Icefields Parkway between Banff and Jasper, but it's well worth tackling some of the region's many hikes – there's something for everyone, whatever your fitness levels – for a real taste of Canada's great outdoors.

BANFF

Banff is the gateway to Banff National Park (➤ 160–163) and the chief town of the four major parks of the Canadian Rockies. It's a busy, bustling place, especially in summer. Beautifully situated astride the Bow River, and in the shadow of the encircling mountains, it makes a pleasant stopover and an essential place for supplies if you're heading deeper into the park. If you're staying, be sure to book rooms well in advance, especially in summer.

The town provides a base for walks and drives in the park, though many people end up browsing the numerous souvenir and outdoor equipment stores in Banff Avenue, the main street. Cafés and good restaurants abound, and the excellent visitor center can point you to a handful of pleasant strolls in and around the town, as well as tour operators who run boating, fishing, riding and rafting trips. Bicycles can also be rented at several outlets.

The town also has three museums: the **Banff Park Museum,** with many stuffed animals indigenous to the park; the **Whyte Museum of the Canadian Rockies,** with displays devoted to the emergence of the Rockies as a tourist destination; and the **Luxton Museum,** home to rather dated displays related to the area's First Nations population. Many people pay a visit to the famous Banff Springs Hotel, and to the **Banff Gondola,** a busy cable car that offers excellent views. Also interesting is the **Cave and Basin National Historic Site,** discovered by three railway laborers in 1883. The reserve created around the hot springs there two years later was the germ of the present national

park. You can also bathe in the **Upper Hot Springs Pool.**

✚ 22G

🛈 224 Banff Avenue ☎ 403/762-2523; www.pc.gc.ca/banff or www.banfflakelouise.com 🕓 Late Jun–Aug daily 8–8; mid-May to late Jun, 1 Sep to mid-Sep 9–7; mid-Sep to mid-May daily 9–5

Banff Park Museum

✉ 93 Banff Avenue ☎ 403/762-1558 🕓 Mid-May to Sep daily 10–6; Oct to mid-May daily 1–5 ✋ Inexpensive

Whyte Museum of the Canadian Rockies

✉ 111 Bear Street ☎ 403/762-2291; www.whyte.org 🕓 Daily 10–5 ✋ Inexpensive

Luxton Museum

✉ 1 Birch Avenue ☎ 403/762-2388; www.buffalonationsmuseum.ca 🕓 Daily 9–6 ✋ Inexpensive

Banff Gondola

✉ Mountain Avenue ☎ 403/762-5438; www.banffgondola.com 🕓 Jan daily 10–4; Feb–Mar daily 10–5; Apr–May daily 8:30–6; Jun–Aug daily 7:30am–9pm; Sep to mid-Oct daily 8:30–6:30; mid-Oct to Nov daily 8:30–4:30; Dec daily 10–4 ✋ Expensive

Cave and Basin National Historic Site

✉ Cave Avenue ☎ 403/762-1566 🕓 Mid-May to Sep daily 9–6; Oct to mid-May Mon–Fri 11–4, Sat–Sun 9:30–5 ✋ Inexpensive ❓ Daily guided tours at 11, 2 and 4 (Sat–Sun only at 11 Oct to mid-May)

Upper Hot Springs Pool

✉ Mountain Avenue ☎ 403/762-1515; www.hotsprings.ca 🕓 Mid-May to early Sep daily 9am–11pm; early Sep to mid-May Sun–Thu 10–10, Fri–Sat 10am–11pm ✋ Moderate

BANFF NATIONAL PARK

Banff National Park is the best-known of the major parks protecting the Canadian Rockies. It began life in 1885 as a small reserve to protect natural hot springs near the present site of Banff, the park's major town (➤ 158–159). In 1887 this became the Rocky Mountains Park, Canada's first national park (and the world's second, after Yellowstone in the United States). The park had a practical as well as environmental purpose, being partly designed to lure visitors, and thus help pay for and promote the government-backed transcontinental railway.

To look at a map of the park today can give the impression that this is a relatively populated area. In fact, there is only one town worthy of the name (Banff), plus Lake Louise (➤ 174–175), a small, modern village and resort 58km (36 miles) north of Banff, to which it is linked by two highways: the Trans-Canada (Hwy 1) and the specially built scenic Bow Valley Parkway. Canmore, just outside the park to the south, is a fast-developing town (➤ 165), but less attractive as a base than Banff or Lake Louise.

A major road, the sublime Icefields Parkway (➤ 44–45), links Lake Louise to Jasper, while the Trans-Canada Highway runs west from Lake Louise to Yoho National Park (➤ 178–180) and Hwy 93 leaves the Trans-Canada Highway midway between Banff and Lake Louise to run through Kootenay National Park (➤ 170–171).

To get the best out of the park, allow at least three days, depending on how keen you are to tackle a hike – there are more than 1,500km (930 miles) of trails to suit all abilities – or pursue other outdoor activities such as biking, riding or golf. The visitor centers at Banff and Lake Louise carry details of all hikes, but the most popular trails can be busy: most of the trailheads (the point from which hikes start) are on the Trans-Canada Highway or Bow Valley Parkways north and south of Banff.

The best easy strolls close to Banff town are Bow Falls Trail (2.4km/1.5 miles), the Hoodoos Trail (10.2km/6.5 miles), Marsh Loop Trail (2.5km/1.5 miles) and Sundance Canyon trail (2km/1.25

miles): distances are round-trip. Standout day hikes are Cory Pass Trail (5.8km/3.6 miles), which involves a tough 915m/3,000ft ascent, but has wonderful views, and Cascade Amphitheatre (13.2km/8 miles, 610m/2,000ft ascent). There are also five major trails off the Bow Valley Parkway, of which the best short walk is the Johnston Canyon Trail (7.4km/4.6 miles, 520m/1,705ft ascent) and the best day hike the Rockbound Lake Trail (16.8km/10.4 miles, 760m/2,493ft ascent). The outstanding walk off Hwy 1 between Banff and Lake Louise is to Bourgeau Lake (15km/9.3 miles, 725m/2,378ft ascent).

Spend one day in and around Banff, which is an obvious base (► 158–159); one (or two) hiking or perhaps rafting on Banff's Bow River, which offers gentle family-friendly trips (more extreme

white-water outings are available on rivers such as Kicking Horse in neighboring Yoho, to which operators will transport you from Banff); and one day perhaps visiting Lake Minnewanka, 10km (6 miles) northeast of Banff, the park's largest lake, where you can take 90-minute **boat tours** and walk or picnic on the banks.

You may then wish to spend a day or two in Lake Louise or Moraine Lake (➤ 48–49), perhaps with excursions into Kootenay National Park (➤ 170–171), and one day driving the Icefields Parkway (➤ 44–45).

✚ 22H 🚊 Banff (➤ 159), Lake Louise (➤ 175)

Lake Minnewanka Boat Tours

☎ 403/762-3473; www.minnewankaboattours.com ⏰ Mid-May to Sep daily 4–5 tours 💰 Expensive

CALGARY

Many visitors come to Calgary expecting to do little but pass through on their way to the Rockies – Banff is just 90 minutes' drive away. In the event, most people find this a fine city, built on revenues from oil and cattle, its glittering downtown skyscrapers rising from the undulating Albertan prairie, its museums and attractive downtown streets – edged by the ice-clear Bow River – well worth a day or more of sightseeing.

Gain an overview of the city, as well as a fantastic view of the Rockies stretched across the western horizon, from the 190m (623ft) **Calgary Tower,** completed in 1968. Also leave plenty of time to wander the shops, cafés and restaurants of 7th Avenue SW and the Eau Claire Market by the river, as well as exploring **Calgary Zoo** (Canada's largest) and **Fort Calgary Historic Park,** site of a stockade built in 1875 to control lawlessness in Canada's pioneer country. Devote most time, however, to the modern **Glenbow Museum,** full of excellent art, and historical and First Nations displays. It's one of western Canada's best museums, second only to Victoria's Royal BC Museum.

✚ 24G

ℹ 200–238 11th Avenue SE ☎ 403/263-8510 or 1-800/661-1678; www.tourismcalgary.com ⚫ Mon–Fri 8–5

Calgary Tower
⊠ Corner of Centre Street and 9th Avenue SW ☎ 403/266-7171;
www.calgarytower.com ⏱ Hours vary seasonally: call for latest details
✋ Moderate

Calgary Zoo
⊠ 1300 Zoo Road NE ☎ 403/232-9300 or 1-800/588-9993;
www.calgaryzoo.org ⏱ Daily 9–6 (last entry 5) ⏱ Expensive

Fort Calgary Historic Park
⊠ 750-9th Ave SE ☎ 403/290-1875; www.fortcalgary.com ⏱ Daily 9–5
✋ Moderate

Glenbow Museum
⊠ 130-9th Avenue SW ☎ 403/268-4100; www.glenbow.org ⏱ Fri–Wed
9–5, Thu 9–9 ✋ Moderate

CANMORE AND KANANASKIS COUNTRY

Kananaskis Country is the name given to a group of beautiful
provincial mountain parks between Calgary and Banff, partly
designed to take some of the pressure off Banff National Park.
Popular with locals, the area has excellent hiking and other
outdoor activities, plus superb winter sports at Nakiska and
Fortress Mountain. Much of the region is accessed via Hwy 40
(off Hwy 1), though one of the busiest areas now centers on
Canmore, 28km (17 miles) from Banff. This booming town has
fewer restrictions on development than its near neighbor and,
while not as beautifully situated, makes a good base, with plenty
of accommodations and innumerable opportunities for outdoor
activities.

✚ 22G and 23G

ℹ 2801 Bow Valley Trail, Canmore
☎ 403/678-5277 or 1-800/
661-8888; www.discoveralberta.
com, www.skinakiska.com,
www.skifortress.com ⏱ Jun–Aug
daily 8–8; Sep–May daily 9–6

ICEFIELDS PARKWAY

Best places to see, ➤ 44–45.

JASPER

Much as Banff is virtually the only
center in Banff National park, so Jasper,
287km (178 miles) north of Banff, is
the only town in Jasper National Park
(➤ 168–169). But where Banff has all
the trappings of a modern town, more
modest Jasper still preserves something
of the gritty, windswept charm of a
frontier settlement. It is, though, an
excellent base, albeit one that is less
spectacularly situated than its southern counterpart.

Like Banff, it owes its existence largely to the railway. First
Nations peoples had used the Yellowhead Pass to the west
across the mountains for centuries, and trappers and traders had
established outposts from about 1810 onward. But it was the
arrival in 1911 of the Grand Trunk Pacific Railway, the country's
second transcontinental railway, that led first to the formation of a
tent city for workers and, eventually, a permanent settlement.

Today, the railway (plus Hwy 16) still runs through the heart
of the town, which collects along two main thoroughfares,
Connaught Drive and Patricia Street. These streets contain plenty
of cafés, restaurants and stores, but also the main park visitor
center and the offices of several tour operators who will organize
hiking and other outdoor activities in and around the town, and in
the park at large. In particular, Jasper is a major rafting base, with
a wide range of trips on the local Athabasca river.

Otherwise the town has little in the way of obvious attractions,
save the small **Yellowhead Museum & Archives,** with displays
devoted to the fur trade and the coming of the railway. The most
obvious excursion is the **Jasper Tramway,** 7km (4 miles) south

of the center, Canada's longest and highest cable car. The car leaves you at a viewpoint and restaurant at 2,285m (7,495ft), with sweeping views and the opportunity to follow an obvious trail (make sure you have suitable clothing and footwear) to the summit of Whistlers Mountain (2,470m/8,104ft).

Also popular are Pyramid and Patricia lakes just north of the town, with lots of easy hiking and picnicking opportunities, plus trips to Maligne Canyon and Maligne Lake (▶ 168–169).

✚ 19L

ℹ 500 Connaught Drive ☎ 780/852-6176; www.pc.gc.ca/jasper

🕔 Jun–Sep daily 9–7; Oct–May daily 9–4

Yellowhead Museum & Archives

✉ 400 Pyramid Lake Road ☎ 780/852-3013; www.jaspermuseum.org

🕔 May–Sep daily 10–5; Oct–Apr Tue–Sun 10–5 💵 Inexpensive

Jasper Tramway

✉ Whistlers Mountain Road ☎ 866/850-8726; www.jaspertramway.com

🕔 Mid-Apr to mid-May, late Aug to mid-Oct daily 10–5; mid-May to late Jun daily 9:30–6:30; late Jun–late Aug daily 9–8. Adverse weather may cause hours to vary 💵 Expensive

JASPER NATIONAL PARK

Jasper National Park tends to be overshadowed by Banff National Park to the south, but it covers a larger and wilder protected area, and is less busy and less commercialized. For keen hikers and campers, the backcountry is more extensive than Banff, with more long-distance trails. And for those who wish to escape some of Banff and Lake Louise's crowds, much of the park has a greater sense of wilderness.

Casual visitors should not be put off, however, for there are plenty of easy trails and manageable day hikes, as well as ways to enjoy the scenery without donning hiking boots. The most obvious is the Icefields Parkway (▶ 44–45), shared with Banff National Park (about half of the road's 230km/143 miles are in the Jasper park), along with scenic roads such as Hwy 16, which runs to the Yellowhead Pass (1,131m/3,711ft), 20km (12.5 miles) west of Jasper town, and then on to Mount Robson Provincial Park (▶ 176). You might also consider taking the majestic VIA Rail (www.viarail.ca) train ride from Jasper to Prince George.

Otherwise, the most popular excursion is a **lake cruise on Maligne Lake,** 48km (30 miles) southwest of Jasper via Maligne Lake Road (companies run tours and shuttle buses along the road if you are without your own transportation). The Rockies' largest natural lake (at 22km/13.5 miles long), Maligne Lake is staggeringly beautiful, and near the lakeshore it's possible to fish, ride and raft, or to rent canoes and row-boats. There are also a couple of easy trails on the east shore of the lake and to the

Schaffer viewpoint (3km/2 miles round-trip). One of the park's best day walks, the Opal Hills Circuit (8.2km/5 miles round-trip, 460m/1,509ft ascent) starts here, from the upper parking area.

En route to or from the lake, you might also explore Maligne Canyon (11km/7 miles from Jasper), a modest but often crowded canyon with short, easy trails. For other walks (including modest strolls), contact the Jasper visitor center: two of the best are Cavell Meadows (3.8km/2.4 miles one-way, 370m/1,213ft ascent), which starts 26km (16 miles) from Jasper town, and the harder Sulphur Skyline (4km/2.5 miles one-way, 700m/2,296ft ascent) from **Miette Hot Springs** (where you can bathe), 55km (34 miles) east of Jasper Town off Hwy 16.

✚ 21K

🛈 500 Connaught Drive, Jasper ☎ 780/852-6176; www.pc.gc.ca/jasper

🕐 Apr to mid-Jun, Oct daily 9–5; mid-Jun to Aug daily 8:30–7; Sep daily 9–6; Nov–Mar daily 9–4

Maligne Lake Cruises

✉ Maligne Tours, 627 Patricia Street, Jasper ☎ 780/852-3370; www.malignelake.com, www.mra.ab.ca 🕐 Departures hourly: ice melt–Jun 4 daily 10–3; Jun 5–24, Sep 4–end of season daily 10–4; Jun 25–Sep 3 daily 10–5 ✋ Expensive

Miette Hot Springs

✉ Miette Road, off Hwy 16, 61km (38 miles) east of Jasper ☎ 780/866-3939 or 1-800/767-1611 🕐 Early May to mid-Jun, Sep to mid-Oct daily 10:30–9; mid-Jun to Aug 8:30am–10:30pm. Closed rest of year

KOOTENAY NATIONAL PARK

Kootenay is the least known of the four major national parks in the Canadian Rockies, and the one most often missed by visitors, many of whom prefer to follow Hwy 1 into Yoho or push on to Jasper along the Icefields Parkway. But not only is it well worth seeing, it is easily visited, a day being sufficient to drive the 200km (124 miles) there and back through the park along Hwy 93 from Castle Junction to Radium Hot Springs. It is a road that offers magnificent views and several hikes, long and short, from trailheads along the way.

The highway climbs quickly from Castle Junction to Vermilion Pass (1,637m/5,370ft), the border with British Columbia and the Continental Divide, the division between the watersheds of rivers that flow to the Atlantic and those that flow to the Arctic or Pacific oceans. Here is the short Fireweed Trail (2km/1.25 miles) into the forest and, 3km (2 miles) beyond, the Stanley Glacier Trail (8.4km/5.2 miles, 365m/1,197ft ascent) for views of the eponymous glacier. Much easier is the stroll along Marble Canyon (0.8km/0.5 miles), 8km (5 miles) from Vermilion Pass, and the nearby walk to the Paint Pots, fascinating old ocher beds once used by the area's earliest inhabitants.

Vermilion Crossing, 20km (12.5 miles) beyond the Paint Pots Trail, is a tiny settlement and the only place to find lodgings, food and fuel in the park. It also has a visitor center and is the start point of several trails. After Kootenay Crossing – a ceremonial spot where the ribbon opening Hwy 93 was cut in 1923 – the road begins to climb, culminating in the Kootenay Valley Viewpoint, with superlative vistas of the Mitchell and Vermilion mountains.

Thereafter, the road drops through Sinclair Canyon toward **Radium Hot Springs,** a sprawling town that takes its name from the park-run natural hot springs (open to the public) on Hwy 93 in the shadow of the canyon.

✉ 21G

ℹ 7556 Main Street East, Radium Hot Springs ☎ 250/347-9505; www. pc.gc.ca/kootenay 🕐 Mid-May to mid-Jun, Sep 1 to mid-Sep daily 9–5; mid-Jun to Aug daily 9–7; mid-Sep to mid-Oct daily 9–4. Closed rest of year

ℹ Kootenay Park Lodge, Vermilion Crossing ☎ 403/762 9196; www. kootenayparklodge.com 🕐 Mid-May to Jun, Sep–early Oct daily 10–5; Jul–Aug daily 9–6. Closed rest of year

Radium Hot Springs
✉ Hwy 93 ☎ 250/347-9485 or 1 800/767-1611; www.hotsprings.ca 🕐 Mid-May to mid-Jun, early Sep to mid-Sep daily 9–5; mid-Jun to early Sep 9–7; mid-Sep to mid-Oct 9–4 ✋ Inexpensive

a drive along the Bow Valley Parkway

Instead of taking Hwy 1 between Banff and Lake Louise, take the parallel Bow Valley Parkway, a specially built scenic road with many points of interest and easy hikes. Drive early to avoid crowds on the trails and for the best chance of seeing wildlife.

Drive west from Banff on Hwy 1 and after 5km (3 miles) take the Bow Valley Parkway exit.

After 3km (2 miles) the Backswamp Lookout offers mountain views and the chance to spot wildlife, including bighorn sheep, beaver, muskrat, osprey and mountain goat. Drive another 3km (2 miles) to the Muleshoe Picnic Area and learn about the park authority's controlled forest-burning program.

After 18km (11 miles) is the trailhead for the easy Johnston Canyon Trail (2.7km/1.7 miles one way).

This is a spectacular but busy trail along a canyon to a pair of impressive waterfalls. Another 3km (2 miles) beyond is Moose Meadows, where you may see grazing elk.

Drive another 5km (3 miles) west and look out for a panel marking the site of Silver City.

Silver City was a shanty town that filled with 3,000 silver miners in 1883, though there never was any silver – unscrupulous local businessmen had started a rumor to make money from prospectors.

After 24km (15 miles) you come to Castle Mountain Junction, with a café, store and fuel station. Drive another 5km (3 miles) past the Rockbound Lake trailhead (8.4km/5.2 miles one-way), Castle Cliffs Viewpoint and Castle Crags trailhead.

This last trail (3.7km/2.3 miles, 520m/1,705ft ascent) is short but steep, climbing above the tree line to offer fine views of the Bow Valley and mountains beyond.

Drive on past Baker Creek to Morant's Curve, about 5km (3 miles) east of Lake Louise. Continue to the end of the Parkway at the Lake Louise Gondola and continue to Lake Louise Village.

Morant's Curve is one of the Rockies' most famous viewpoints, thanks to a panorama that embraces the railway and a broad sweep of the mountains.

Distance 52km (32 miles)
Time 1–5 hours depending on stops and hikes
Start point Banff ✚ 22G
End point Lake Louise ✚ 21H
Lunch Baker Creek Bistro (➤ 70) or Lake Louise Village
🅷 Banff (➤ 159), Lake Louise (➤ 175)

LAKE LOUISE

Lake Louise is the second center in Banff National Park after Banff, and divides into two parts. Just off the main Hwy 1 is Lake Louise Village, a small purpose-built area comprising a handful of shops, park visitor center, hotels, a youth hostel and cafés. From here, Lake Louise Drive winds 4.5km (2.8 miles) and climbs 200m (655ft) to Lake Louise, one of the most famous sights in the Rockies. On the lakeshore stands the Chateau Lake Louise hotel, a vast high-rise that anywhere else might be a blight on the landscape, but which here is dwarfed by the extraordinary grandeur of the lake and its forest and glacier-hung

mountains. The lakefront is invariably extremely busy, so visit early if possible. Easy trails follow the lake shore, or you can climb to Lake Agnes (where there is a Teahouse for refreshments), a very popular 3.4km (2-mile) walk with 300m (984ft) of ascent.

This can be combined with other trails to reach the head of the valley above the lake. You can also rent canoes to take on the lake. Across the Bow Valley, a short way northeast of Lake Louise Village, is the **Lake Louise Gondola,** a cable car that runs to a superb viewpoint at 2,088m (6,850ft).

✉ 21H

ℹ Lake Louise Village ☎ 403/522-3833; www.pc.gc.ca 🕔 Jan–Apr, Oct–Dec daily 9–4; May to mid-Jun and Sep 14–30 daily 9–5; mid-Jun to early Sep daily 9–8; early Sep–Sep 13 daily 9–7

Lake Louise Gondola

☎ 403/522-3555 or 1-800/258-7669; www.lakelouisegondola.com 🕔 Mid-May to mid-Jun, early Sep–Sep 30 daily 9–4:30; mid-Jun to early Sep daily 9–5 💵 Expensive

MORAINE LAKE

Best places to see, ➤ 48–49.

MOUNT ROBSON

Mount Robson is the highest point in the Canadian Rockies (3,954m/12,973ft), and is protected by a provincial park that borders Jasper National Park to the west. One of the mountain's many beauties is that in good weather its colossal outlines can be seen from the road, Hwy 16, which runs from Jasper, about 60km (37 miles) to the east. In the first 24km (15 miles) of highway from Jasper, to the border of British Columbia and the Mount Robson Provincial Park, the road (shadowed by the railway) climbs to the Yellowhead Pass (1,131m/3,711ft). If the scenery here seems relatively tame, the view of Mount Robson, when it comes, is breathtaking, partly because the mountain stands in isolation, and partly because its monumental south face – a sheer rise of some 3,100m (10,171ft) – presents itself to the viewer (pick a clear day for your trip). There is a seasonal visitor center near the viewpoint, plus a café and garage nearby, but very few other facilities, so stock up in Jasper. You can return to Jasper, or continue south or west on highways 5 or 16, both extremely scenic drives.

✚ 18M

🛈 Hwy 16 ☎ 250/566-4325; www.elp.gov.bc.ca/bcparks ⏰ Jun, Sep daily 8–5; Jul–Aug daily 8–8. Closed rest of the year

WATERTON LAKES NATIONAL PARK

Waterton is the Cinderella of the Rockies' national parks, but only because it occupies a region close to the US border that is difficult to incorporate on any logical tour of Alberta and British Columbia. On the ground, the mountain scenery, the hiking (with 255km/ 158 miles of excellent trails) and other outdoor activities

are just as good as in the four better-known parks to the north. The park, which dates from 1895, centers on the small town of Waterton, prettily situated on the shores of Upper Waterton Lake. Waterton contains most of the park's accommodations, services and tours, with lots of hiking from, or close to the town, plus boat trips on the lake. Two scenic roads run west from Waterton into the heart of the park, the Akamina Parkway, which leads 20km

(12.5 miles) to Cameron Lake (walk back to Waterton on the sublime Carthew-Alderson Trail: 19km/11.8 miles, 612m/2,007ft ascent), and the Red Rock Canyon Parkway, which runs 15km (9.3 miles) to the mouth of the eponymous canyon.

➕ 22G (off map)

ℹ Entrance Road ☎ 403/859-5133; www.pc.gc.ca/watertonlakes ⏱ Early May–early Oct daily 8–7

YOHO NATIONAL PARK

Yoho takes its name from a Cree First Nations word meaning "wonder," testament to the majesty of the scenery in a national park many believe is the superior of both its neighbors, Banff and Jasper. Much smaller than these more famous parks, it lies wholly in British Columbia, bisected by the Trans-Canada Highway (Hwy 1) and home to just one village, Field, 28km (17.5 miles) west of Lake Louise.

The presence of the road makes it easy to breeze through the park admiring the scenery from a car or bus (the railway also shadows the road, but it no longer carries public services). As ever, though, it is well worth lingering, perhaps spending the day here before returning to Lake Louise or Banff, where there are far more accommodations options.

Two side roads north from the Trans-Canada offer access to the park's interior. The first leaves the highway about 3km (1.8 miles) east of Field, just after the Lower Spiral Tunnel Lookout, a viewpoint that offers views of the exits and entrances to the railway's famous Spiral Tunnels. These are two figure-of-eight galleries built in the 1880s to help the line negotiate the region's 4 percent gradients, then the steepest of any commercial railway in North America. Time it right and you can see the last box cars of freight trains entering a tunnel as their locomotive emerges close by.

The side road runs 9km (5.6 miles) up the Yoho Valley, coming to a dead end near Takkakaw Falls, one of the park's highlights. Taking their name from the Cree word for "magnificent," the falls are 245m (804ft) high, making them one of Canada's highest waterfalls (Niagara Falls are 52m/170ft high). Several hiking trails leave from the waterfalls' parking area, including the easy Point Lace Falls (1.9km/1.2 miles one-way, minimum ascent) and Laughing Falls (3.8km/2.3 miles, 60m/197ft ascent). Also extremely popular is the Twin Falls Trail (8.5km/5.3 miles one-way, 290m/951ft ascent).

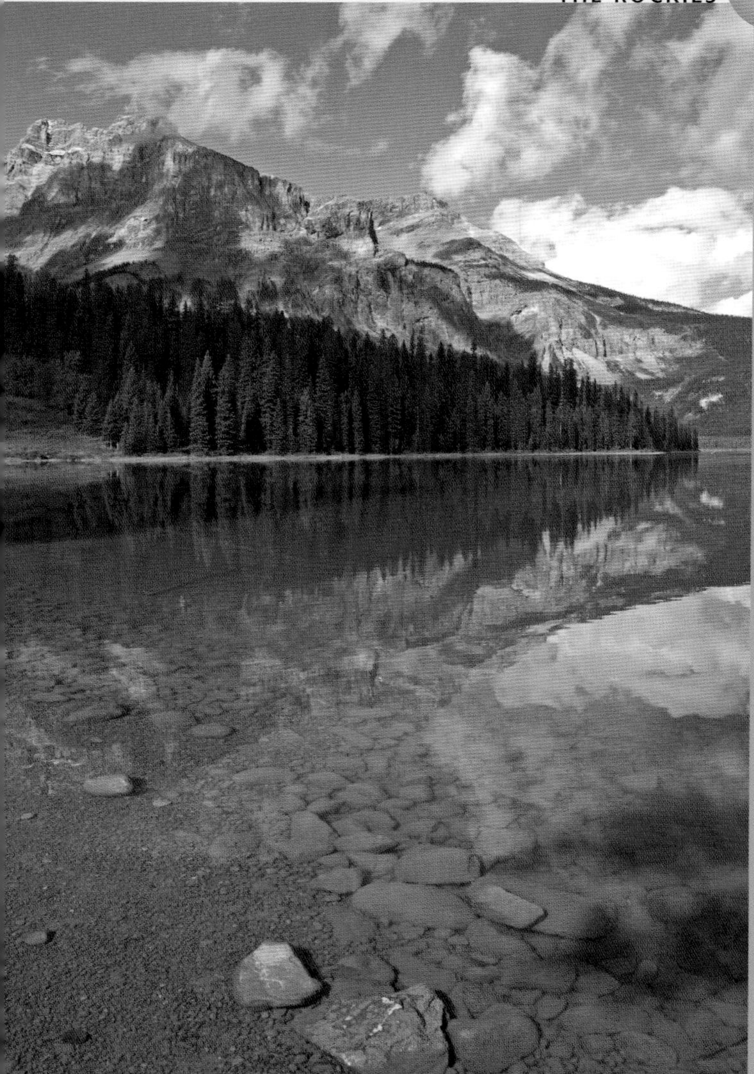

The Yoho Pass trail (10.9km/6.7 miles, 310m/1,017ft ascent, 510m/1,673ft descent) crosses west and drops down to Emerald Lake, which can also be reached by the second of the side roads off the Trans-Canada, 2km (1.2 miles) west of Field. This is home to the Emerald Lake Lodge, one of the Rockies' premier hotels, as well as a network of trails, including an easy (and wheelchair-accessible) nature trail (4.6km/2.8 miles round trip), Hamilton Falls (1.6km/1 mile round trip) and Hamilton Lake (5.5km/3.4 miles one-way, 850m/2,788ft ascent).

A third area, Lake O'Hara, can also be approached by road, but here there are stringent quota systems (apply online or to the visitor center for details), making casual visits difficult.

Field and the Burgess Shales

The tiny village of Field began life as a railway construction camp in 1884. It has guesthouses, a park visitor center and a hotel. It is also the base for guided tours of the **Burgess Shales,** a UNESCO World Heritage Site. The shales are layers of sedimentary rock riddled with the fossils of 120 types of soft-bodied creatures from the Middle Cambrian period (515–530 million years ago), one of only three places in the world where such fossils are found. Note that tours must be pre-booked and involve quite tough climbs of over 700m (2,300ft).

✚ 21H

ℹ Hwy 1, Field ✉ 250/343-6783; www.pc.gc.ca/yoho ⏰ Jan–Apr, late Sep–Dec daily 9–4; May to mid-Jun, Sep 1–late Sep daily 9–5; mid-Jun to Aug daily 9–7

Yoho-Burgess Shale Foundation

☎ 1/800/343-3006 (Mon–Fri 10–3); www.burgess-shale.bc.ca ⏰ Guided tours Jul to mid-Sep

HOTELS

BANFF

⚇⚇⚇ Buffalo Mountain Lodge ($$)

Banff has many comfortable in-town options, but the detached lodges here are just out of town in a pretty rural setting and have unusually chic interiors.

✉ 700 Tunnel Mountain Drive ☎ 403/762-7417 or 1-800/661-1367; www.crmr.com

⚇⚇⚇ The Juniper ($$)

A boutique hotel that breaks the mold of most older and predictable Banff hotels, with adjacent chalets with pared-down, contemporary interiors. It is close to the foot of Mount Norquay.

✉ 1 Juniper Way ☎ 403/762-2281; www.thejuniper.com

⚇⚇ Red Carpet Inn ($)

This is one of several good, basic and older motels on the main road into Banff from the Trans-Canada Highway (Hwy 1).

✉ 425 Banff Avenue ☎ 403/762-4184 or 1-800/563-4609; www.banfffredcarpet.com

CALGARY

⚇⚇⚇ Sandman Hotel Downtown Calgary ($$)

Hotels in the Sandman chain are reliable and this 300-room, high-rise hotel is Calgary's first-choice mid-range lodgings.

✉ 888-7th Avenue SW ☎ 403/237-8626 or 1-800/726-3626; www.sandmanhotels.com

JASPER

⚇⚇ Becker's Chalets ($$)

This is the nicest of the out-of-town lodges and cabins near Jasper, with 96 one-, two- and three-bedroom cabins. Most cabins have wood-burning stoves and kitchen facilities.

✉ 5km (3 miles) south of Jasper on Hwy 93 South ☎ 780/852-3779; www.beckerschalets.com

�596�596 Lobstick Lodge ($$)

This is the best of several hotels at the northern edge of Jasper, thanks to its indoor pool and its large, if simply furnished rooms (ask for rooms on upper floors); some rooms have kitchenettes.

✉ 94 Geikie Street ☎ 780/852-4431 or 1-888/852-7737; www.mtn-park-lodges.com

LAKE LOUISE
�596�596 Lake Louise Inn ($$)

Rooms are always hard to come by in Lake Louise, so while this hotel is conventional and straightforward, it has the advantage of being large and in a convenient location in Lake Louise Village.

✉ 210 Village Road ☎ 403/522-3791 or 1-800/661-9237; www.lakelouiseinn.com

�596�596 �596� Post Hotel & Spa ($$$)

The Fairmont Chateau Lake Louise is the luxury choice on Lake Louise itself, but the riverside Post is the best hotel in Lake Louise village, with a wide range of room types and facilities.

✉ 200 Pipestone Road, Lake Louise Village ☎ 403/522-3989 or 1-800/661-1586; www.posthotel.com

YOHO NATIONAL PARK
Cathedral Mountain Chalets ($$–$$$)

These 21 luxury chalets occupy a lovely mountain setting just off the Trans-Canada Highway, near the junction for the road to Takkawaw Falls, making this an ideal and very comfortable base.

✉ Trans-Canada Highway, 4km (2.5 miles) east of Field ☎ 250/343-6442 or 1-866/619-6442; www.cathedralmountain.com

Kicking Horse Lodge ($$)

Field has several small guesthouses, but only one hotel, the Kicking Horse Lodge, which has pleasant if unremarkable cabin-style rooms and the lively Roundhouse Pub and Grill downstairs. Value family rooms with kitchens sleep up to six.

✉ 100 Centre Street, Field ☎ 250/343-6303 or 1-800/659-4944; www.kickinghorselodge.net

RESTAURANTS

BANFF

✦✦ Baker Creek Bistro ($$–$$$)
See page 70.

✦✦ Cilantro Mountain Café ($)
This informal restaurant centers on a large wood-fired pizza oven, but the menu also features pastas and more adventurous (but well-priced) steaks, game and chicken dishes. In summer you can eat out on the pleasant terrace.
✉ Buffalo Mountain Lodge, 700 Tunnel Mountain Road ☎ 403/762-2400
🕐 Daily 5–10pm. Closed Mon–Tue in winter

✦✦ Coyote's Deli and Grill ($)
A small, informal bustling café and grill offering great breakfasts, coffee, cakes and snacks to take out, but also fuller meals that include pastas, pizza and Cajun- and Mexican-influenced dishes.
✉ 206 Caribou Street ☎ 403/762-3963 🕐 Daily 7am–11pm

✦✦✦ Saltlik ($$)
A contemporary steakhouse, serving sublime Albertan beef in a stylish dining room distinguished by murals, mood lighting and wood floors. Start with a drink at the semicircular bar, then after dinner, drop down to the Lik Lounge, a sleek but expensive bar and club.
✉ 221 Bear Street ☎ 403/762-2467 🕐 Daily 11am–2am

CALGARY

✦✦ Earls ($–$$)
Earls is part of a reliable and stylish chain, offering a wide range of well-cooked dishes from a variety of cuisines (Asian to Italian to North American) in informal surroundings and with pleasant service.
✉ 315 8th Avenue SW ☎ 403/265-3275 🕐 Daily 11–11

✦✦✦ River Café ($$)
See page 71.

JASPER

▽▽▽ Andy's Bistro ($$–$$$)

One of the best places for a treat and fine dining in Jasper, serving refined food that embraces Asian, Indian – even Swiss – cuisine.

✉ 606 Patricia Street ☎ 780/852-4559 ⏰ Daily 5–10pm

▽ Bear's Paw Bakery ($)

Many locals come here for the coffee, home-baked bread and cakes and take-out sandwiches, or for high-calorie treats to take out on the trail.

✉ 4 Cedar Avenue ☎ 780/852-3233; www.bearspawbakery.com ⏰ Mon–Thu 6–6, Fri–Sun 6am–9pm

▽ Papa George's ($$)

Papa George's opened in 1924, and though it may not be much to look at, it has long been a locals' favorite, thanks to its varied and first-rate menu and generous portions. Breakfast and lunch are especially good value.

✉ 404 Connaught Drive ☎ 780/852-3351 ⏰ Daily 7–2:30, 5–9:30 or later

LAKE LOUISE

▽▽▽ Deer Lodge Dining Room ($–$$$)

The restaurant of the Post Hotel & Spa (► 182) offers the best quality dining in Lake Louise Village, but closer to the lake, the Mount Fairview Dining Room at Deer Lodge is the place for traditional meat, fish and game dishes. Less formal dining (plus afternoon teas), with superb views of the Victoria Glacier, is available in the Caribou Lounge.

✉ 109 Lake Louise Drive ☎ 403/522-3991; www.crmr.com ⏰ Dining Room breakfast and dinner daily, lounge daily 11–11

▽▽ Lake Louise Station ($$–$$$)

Dining with a difference, either in what was formerly Lake Louise's main railway station building (dating from 1909) – with Canadian cuisine in an informal setting – or more adventurous cooking in a beautifully restored Delamere railway dining car.

✉ 200 Sentinel Road ☎ 403/522-2600 ⏰ Daily 11:30am–midnight

SHOPPING

Not many visitors come to the Canadian Rockies with the expectation of good shopping. However, there is one retail area in which the region excels, and that is in stores selling outdoor clothing and equipment. This is especially true of Banff, where there are dozens of such shops, offering excellent choices, but not necessarily the keenest prices. If you are serious about purchasing outdoor gear, and have time in Calgary, then be sure to visit the excellent Mountain Equipment Co-op (830 10th Avenue SW, tel: 403/269-2420; www.mec.ca), sister store to the company's vast shop in Vancouver. Canmore and Jasper also have plenty of outdoor equipment outlets (though fewer than Banff), but otherwise most of the Rockies' towns offer little more than souvenir stores and the odd arts and crafts gallery. For general shopping, Calgary is the best bet, with the excellent Eau Claire Market for specialist stores and Stephen Avenue and other malls on and around 8th Avenue SW in downtown for general goods.

ENTERTAINMENT

All the Rockies centers have large young (and often expat) workforces, plus lots of winter sports enthusiasts in search of après-ski fun. As a result, there is a surprisingly lively nightlife scene, as well as a succession of cultural events. In Banff, look for events connected with the Banff Festival during the summer and check with visitor centers for other current events.

Banff has plenty of hotel and other lounges with bars and occasional live music. Try Tommy's (120 Banff Avenue, tel: 403/762-8888), a British-style neighborhood pub, or St. James's Gate (207 Wolf Street, tel: 403/762-9355; www.stjamesgatebanff.com), with regular live music. The Hoodoo Lounge (137 Banff Avenue, tel: 403/760-8636; www.hoodoolounge.com), the town's largest club, or nearby and co-owned Aurora (110 Banff Avenue, tel: 403/760 5300; www.aurorabanff.com), are the places to dance.

In Jasper, the Jasper Brewing Company (624 Connaught Street, tel: 780/852-4111; www.jasperbrewingco.com), is the best place for an evening drink.

Index

Acknowledgments

The Automobile Association would like to thank the following photographers, companies and picture libraries for their assistance in the preparation of this book.

Abbreviations for the picture credits are as follows – (t) top; (b) bottom; (c) centre; (l) left; (r) right; (AA) AA World Travel Library.

4l Rosemary Rock, Jasper NP, AA/J Tims; 4c Coal Harbour float plane, AA/J Tims; 4r Butchart Gardens, AA/C Sawyer; 5l Kits beach, AA/J Tims; 5r Canada Place, AA/C Sawyer; 6/7 Jasper NP, AA/J Tims; 8/9 Granville Island, AA/C Sawyer; 10/11t Canada Place, AA/C Coe; 10 Gastown, AA/C Sawyer; 10/1b Emerald Lake, Yoho NP, AA/J Tims; 11t Parliament Buildings, Victoria, AA/J Tims; 11b Burrard Inlet and Downtown Vancouver, AA/P Timmermans; 12 Chinatown, AA/J Tims; 13tl Granville Island, AA/J Tims; 13tc Granville Island, AA/M Dent; 13tr Granville Island, AA/J Tims; 13b Hamburger Mary's, AA/J Tims; 14t Water Street Café, Gastown, AA/J Tims; 14b Milestones Grill and Bar, Yaletown, AA/J Tims; 15l Raincity Grill, AA/J Tims; 15r Inniskillin Vineyard, AA/J Tims; 16 Chinatown, AA/J Tims; 16/7 Skyride gondola, Grouse Mountain, AA/C Sawyer; 17 Granville Island market, AA/C Sawyer; 18t Thunderbird Totem Poles outside Royal British Columbia Museum, AA/J Tims; 18b Icefields Parkway, AA/C Sawyer; 19t Nelson, AA/C Sawyer; 19b Banff NP, AA/J Tims; 20/1 Coal Harbour float plane, AA/J Tims; 24/5 Chinese New Year, AA/J Tims; 26/7 Sky Train, AA/J Tims; 27 Bus, AA/M Dent; 34/5 Butchart Gardens, AA/C Sawyer; 36/7, 37tr and 37b Butchart Gardens, AA/J Tims; 37tl Butchart Gardens, AA/C Sawyer; 38 Canada Place, AA/C Sawyer; 39 Canada Place, AA/J Tims; 40t, 40c and 40b Granville Island, AA/J Tims; 41 View over Granville Island, AA/J Tims; 42/3 Grouse Mountain, AA/P Timmermans; 43 Grouse Mountain, AA/J Tims; 44/5 Bow Lake, Banff NP, AA/J Tims; 45t Icefields Parkway, AA/P Bennett; 45b Parker Ridge Trek, Jasper NP, AA/J Tims; 46/7 Kootenay Lake, AA/C Sawyer; 47 Kootenay NP, AA/J Tims; 48/9 Moraine Lake, AA/C Sawyer; 49t and 49b Moraine Lake, AA/J Tims; 50 and 51t Museum of Anthropology, AA/J Tims; 51b Museum of Anthropology, AA/P Bennett; 52/3t and 52/3b Royal British Columbia Museum, Victoria, AA/J Tims; 53 Royal British Columbia Museum, AA/M Dent; 54 Stanley Park Flower Garden, AA/J Tims; 54/5 City skyline from Stanley Park sea wall, AA/P Bennett; 56/7 Kits beach, AA/J Tims; 58/9 View from Vancouver Lookout, AA/J Tims; 60/1 Black Bear, Jasper NP, AA/J Tims; 62t Science World, AA/J Tims; 62b Lynn Canyon Park suspension bridge, AA/J Tims; 62/3 Stanley Park Aquarium, AA/C Sawyer; 64/5 Kits beach, AA/J Tims; 66/7 Parker Ridge Trek, Jasper NP, AA/J Tims; 68 Stanley Park, AA/P Bennett; 69 Johnston Canyon, Banff NP, AA/J Tims; 71t Bishops Restaurant, AA/J Tims; 71c Chinatown Night Market, AA/J Tims; 71b Bishops Restaurant, AA/J Tims; 72/3 Vancouver Art Gallery, AA/J Tims; 74/5 Canada Place, AA/C Sawyer; 78 and 79r Capilano Suspension Bridge, AA/J Tims; 79l Capilano Salmon Hatchery, AA/J Tims; 80 Dr Sun Yat Sen Gardens, AA/J Tims; 81 Chinatown Night Market, AA/J Tims; 82 Coal Harbour waterfront buildings, AA/J Tims; 83 Inuit sculpture, English Bay, AA/P Timmermans; 84 Gastown shop, AA/J Tims; 85 Steam-powered Clock, Gastown, AA/J Tims; 86/7t Galiano Island, AA/J Tims; 86/7b View from ferry to Galiano Island, AA/J Tims; 88 Vancouver Museum, AA/J Tims; 89 Lighthouse Park, AA/J Tims; 90/1 Downtown from Lonsdale Quay, AA/J Tims; 91 Lynn Canyon Park, AA/J Tims; 92 Marine Building, AA/J Tims; 93 View to Mount Baker from Mount Seymour Prov Park AA/P Bennett; 94/5 Queen Elizabeth Park, AA/J Tims; 96 Science World, AA/J Tims; 97t Vancouver Aquarium, AA/J Tims; 97b Vancouver Aquarium, AA/C Sawyer; 98/9 Christ Church Cathedral, AA/J Tims; 100t Emily Carr's 'Rhythm of Nature' (1937), Vancouver Art Gallery, AA/C Sawyer; 100b Landscape painting by Emily Carr, Vancouver Art Gallery, AA/C Coe; 101 View from Vancouver Lookout, AA/J Tims; 102/3 Maritime Museum, AA/J Tims; 103 Vancouver Public Library, AA/J Tims; 105 Coal Harbour waterfront buildings, AA/J Tims; 106 Sakana Bistro, Yaletown, AA/J Tims; 117 Float plane, Inner Harbour AA/J Tims; 118 Art Gallery of Greater Victoria, AA/J Tims; 118/9 Beacon Hill Park, AA/J Tims; 121 Market Square entrance, AA/P Bennett; 122 Craigdarroch Castle, AA/J Tims; 123 Helmcken House, AA/J Tims; 124/5 Empress Hotel, AA/J Tims; 126 Lighthouse lamp outside Maritime Museum, AA/J Tims; 127 Old Town, AA/J Tims; 128 Parliament Buildings, AA/P Timmermans; 129 Parliament Buildings, AA/J Tims; 130t and 130b Point Ellice House and Gardens National Historic Site, © Ceara Lorie, Point Ellice House and Gardens National Historic Site; 131 and 132 Whale-watching, AA/J Tims; 137 Marina, Lake Okanagan, Kelowna, AA/C Sawyer; 138/9 and 139 Fraser Canyon, AA/J Tims; 140/1 View from Abbott Ridge, Glacier NP © Getty Images/All Canada Photos/Kurt Werby; 142 View from Highway 3, AA/J Tims; 142/3 Highway 3, AA/J Tims; 144/5 Autumn view of town from Gyro Park in Nelson, Photolibrary; 146/7 Balsam Lake, Mount Revelstoke NP, AA/J Tims; 148/9 Sunrise over Kamloops Lake, Kamloops, © Getty Images/All Canada Photos/Kelly Funk; 149 Highway 3, Okanagan, AA/J Tims; 150/1 Shuswap Lake, AA/J Tims; 151 Wells Gray Provincial Park, AA/J Tims; 152 Chairlift, Whistler, AA/P Bennett; 157 Emerald Lake, Yoho NP, AA/J Tims; 158 Banff town and 159, AA/J Tims; 160/1 Peyto Lake, Icefields Parkway, Banff NP, AA/J Tims; 162/3 Lake Louise, Banff NP, AA/J Tims; 163 Bighorn sheep, AA/J Tims; 164 Calgary, AA/P Bennett; 165 View over Canmore, AA/J Tims; 166 and 167 Jasper town, AA/J Tims; 168/9 Patricia Lake, Jasper NP, AA/J Tims; 170 and 171 Vermillion River, Kootenay NP, AA/P Bennett; 172/3 Bow Valley Parkway, AA/P Bennett; 174/5 Lake Louise, Banff NP, AA/J Tims; 176 Mount Robson, AA/C Sawyer; 177t Cameron Lake, Waterton Lakes NP, AA/P Bennett; 177b Buffalo, Waterton Lakes NP, AA/P Bennett; 179 Emerald Lake, Yoho NP, AA/J Tims; 180 Fossil, trilobite, Burgess Shale, © Tony Waltham/Robert Harding.

Every effort has been made to trace the copyright holders, and we apologise in advance for any accidental errors. We would be happy to apply any corrections in the following edition of this publication.

Sight locator index

This index relates to the maps on the covers. We have given map references to the main sights in the book. Grid references in italics indicate sights featured on the town plans. Some sights within towns may not be plotted on the maps.